FIGURE/GROUND

FIGURE/GROUND

A DESIGN COVERSATION with SCOTT JOHNSON and BILL FAIN

MORRIS NEWMAN, Editor
Introduction by JOSEPH GIOVANNINI

Balcony Press, Los Angeles

BALCONY PRESS

First Edition

PUBLISHED IN THE UNITED STATES OF AMERICA BY BALCONY PRESS 2003
Design LORRAINE WILD and STUART SMITH, LOS ANGELES
Printing and production PACE+NAVIGATOR, CITY OF INDUSTRY, CALIFORNIA

FIGURE/GROUND © 2003 BALCONY PRESS

Library of Congress Catalog Card Number: 2003111805
ISBN 1-890449-23-7

IMAGE CREDITS
All images credit Johnson Fain unless otherwise noted.
Andy Warhol Foundation for the Visual Arts/ARS, NY; MOCA, Los Angeles: 29; AP/Wide
World Photos: 61; Benny Chan: Front Cover, 19R, 148, 150, 176, 204, 216, 218, 219, 220,
224, 108–109, 146–147, 174–175, 18R, 214–215; Brazilian Tourism Board: 29; Charles
Le Noir: 237R, 237L; Denise Applewhite, Courtesy Princeton University: M. Christine
Boyer, 99; Erhard Pfeiffer: 11R, 17R, 22–23, 27, 55, 70–71, 72, 74, 75, 76, 104, 116, 118,
119, 124, 126, 127, 132, 134, 156, 157, 158, 178, 179, 180, 226, 227, 100–101, 114–115,
122–123, 130–131, 200–201, 222–223; Erich Koyama: 185; Imago-Terrae: 181;
James Leynse: Jacques Derrida, 85; John Cleese: 217; John Deeb: Sam Rivers, 133;
John Louie: Moscone Center, 111; John Nikolai: 25; Jon Messer: 44, 52, 82–83,
86–87, 138–139, 170–171, 172, 206–207; Kirk Irwin: 152–153; Lawrence Perron: 17L,
42–43, 46, 47, 50; Luxor Hotel, Las Vegas: 35; Mark Defeo: 110, 144; Mark Lohman: 48,
72, 110, 154, 160–161, 166; Mary E. Nichols: 11L, 30; Mike Toy: 56–57, 58, 59; Mitchell
Photographics: 172; Museum Associates/LACMA: 155; Norman Kondy: 112–113,
164, 165; Piatt Associates: 144; Richard Payne: 99; Roger Gordey. Courtesy C.F. Peters
Corporation. EMF Archives: John Cage, 133; Ron Campise. Courtesy Los Angeles
Department of Recreation and Parks: 193; Roy Export Company Establishment: 205;
SONY Berlin/P. Adenis: Sony Center, 111; Steve Whittaker: 81; Tim Street Porter:
24, 26, 102, 105, 106; Tom Bonner: 92–93, 94, 95, 96, 97, 120; UNLV Photo Services,
Geri Kodey, Photographer: Dave Hickey, 85; Volker Corell: Terminal Post Office Annex,
81; William H. Fain, Jr.: Back Cover, 182, 183, 194, 195, 198, 199; Yan Gen: 62–63

CONTENTS

RECONSTRUCTED MODERNISTS

Joseph Giovannini

The scope and scale of Johnson Fain's practice—
from houses in Napa to the Central Business District
of Beijing and the world's tallest skyscraper—would
give Baron Haussman and Robert Moses pause.
Many architects maintain a boutique practice, and
many urban planners specialize in thinking big.
But few firms reconcile poles of scale ranging "from
the spoon to the city," in the phrase of Italian
Modernist Ernesto Rogers. Experts in the high rise,
principals Scott Johnson and William Fain diversified
their practice in the early 1990s branching out to
office campuses, country clubs, university buildings,
wineries and parking garages. They also expanded
the breadth of their expertise. The architects became
anthropologists in their research for a Native
American center in Oklahoma and religious scholars
for a monastic retreat in Southern California. They
acted as environmentalists in their design of one of
the most energy-conscious projects ever built in
the United States—several city blocks facing the capitol
building in Sacramento. In an era when specialists
have difficulty generating larger visions, the architects
have pursued the whole.

Johnson Fain's practice is a terrain of cultural syn-
thesis beyond form: they cultivate rather than repress
the subtleties and complexities of a commission.
The two principals evolved their position after living
through several turbulent cycles of architectural
style and theory. Both studied at Harvard's Graduate
School of Design in the mid-1970s, when Le Corbusier
Modernists espoused universal truths that implied
solutions types for the normative Modular Man. Those
purist theologies were soon challenged first by historical Postmodernists and then by Deconstructivists.
Johnson and Fain, like everyone else building a professional psyche in their architectural generation,
confronted the classicizing projects of Michael Graves
in the 1970s and then the post-classical Decon-
structivist counter-revolution in the late 1980s. By
the 1990s, after more than a decade of turmoil
challenging the fundamentals once assumed at
Harvard's GSD, the architects had to determine their
identities without mimicry and without retrenching
in the neo-conservative Modernist revival that emerged
as the fall-back position for many other designers.

Compounding the concept wars that swept the
profession was Johnson and Fain's own more
local confrontation with the practice they eventually
took over. Johnson Fain is the successor firm to
Pereira Associates, named after one of the Southern

California's most successful post-War practitioners. Like many other Modernists of his generation, William Pereira believed in the power of pure form to define a building and the power of geometry to organize a site. At the University of California at Irvine, for example, he created a campus plan based on the wheel, its hub, and radial spokes. In 1987, when Johnson and Fain modified the plan, they were addressing the soul of their own firm, growing the seeds of a generational shift. The two architects created a pedestrian street with a tangential relationship to the wheel's circle. Rather than pure Euclidean forms organizing space within the wheel and hub, they grafted a simple walking street at the edge of the campus, creating a sense of contained space between the two walls of buildings, and a sense of place that encouraged and sustained pedestrian activity. They took the campus back from geometry as they urbanized a suburban site and gave pedestrians a field of experience much denser than the loosely defined, leftover spaces within the wheel. At Irvine, the new whole was a composite based on an urbanistic complexity never admitted in Pereira's practice. Johnson and Fain had performed an Oedipal operation on their professional legacy.

As the principals of Johnson Fain developed their own independent voice in the late 1980s and early 1990s, the two escaped not only the shadow of their near father figure but also that of the more distant historic figures. Modernism was the lingua franca of their generation and abstraction remained the basis of their aesthetic. But they were not content simply to return to Modernism as archivists, and instinctively

chose to expand its assumptions, evolving the language of abstraction toward complexity rather than simplicity. They would no longer be reductive: in their interest in creating lively, humanist environments, they would not reduce a campus to the geometry of a wheel. The redirection and redefinition of their practice amounted to a critique of historic Modernism and the status of a building as an absolute object, with its meanings contained in its own form. Their path out of a reductive and restrictive theory of practice, especially one labeled as corporate, was to expand content beyond form. They invented their way beyond their received practice and the received wisdom of the field to a reconstructed Modernism.

The complexity they have developed is not complexity as a style, but complexity that is a registration of research. The architects are interested in cultural connections on a deep level, not semiotic symbols flagging putative meaning like semaphores. Formal purities melt down as they make visible and physical connections to the city, to nature, and the larger culture. Instead of being objects isolated in the infinities of Modernist space, their buildings and urban designs open to the culture and to physical space conceived as active and specific rather than passive and undifferentiated. When they came into their own as principals of Johnson Fain, they escaped the shadow of the father figure, and escaped, too, the urge to draw on the vocabularies developed by other paternal figures in more distant corners of the profession. The architects achieved their own identity through a synthetic process of design in an expanded referential field.

8

Scott Johnson cites jazz composition as an analogue for how he designs, referring to the overall musical structure and the variations that grow from it. Johnson says, "We are talking about a conception of beauty which in some way is a product of a dialectic between structure and improvisation." Even with tall buildings, perhaps the most recalcitrant and monolithic building type, Johnson breaks the rules, elaborating surfaces, building up layers. In his most recent high rise design, for the MGM tower in Los Angeles' Century City, he ruptures the gridded facade to spatialize the surfaces and wrest depth from the flat wall. At the entrance, he segments space with one broad circular arc that celebrates the sense of entry.

For Johnson, regularity—regardless of its exact geometric persuasion—is an open-ended rather than closed armature that allows mending and exceptions. He relaxes structure and violates purity; his designs oscillate in an unstable space between the general and specific, the universal and local, always resisting the resolution of stasis.

Author of a complex 140-story skyscraper conceived to consummate the skyline of the Central Business District in Beijing, Johnson designs large structures that have complex agendas. But his smaller buildings, particularly his own houses, provide the clearest index of his architectural intentions.

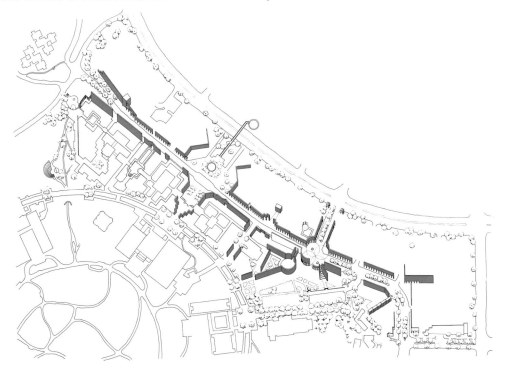

"Main Street", University of California at Irvine

For his vacation home in Napa, on a site with rolling vineyards and forever views, Johnson protected the interior from the nearby road by creating a double line-up of closed cubes whose backs face the street: each cube contains a room. Johnson drives an axial promenade from the front door straight through the line-up of rooms. With Hitchcockian suspense, the blinded hallway steps down the slope to a spacious, glass-lined living room that opens onto an expansive terrace facing the panorama. Johnson here proves to be the master of sequence, starting with the compressed entrance and ending with the thrusting release into the view. The house delivers the family to the out-of-doors through the vector of its interior space.

The house is highly structured—linear and roughly bilaterally symmetrical—but on either side of the passage, there are events, such as side windows and pockets for seating, as the walls push and pull back and forth, an exercise in spatial breathing. The corridor may be linear but Johnson riffed the straight line to create a corridor that is laterally porous and episodic.

Johnson starts with a strong structuring idea that he relaxes locally; he elaborates the basic 5-bedroom program by exploiting in plan small spatial opportunities and casual moments. The informal formality achieves a greater warmth through Johnson's haptic material palette that exhibits a range of textures and includes concrete block, smooth flagstone, slate tiles, plywood paneling, hand applied white-gold leaf, and exposed wood joists, complete with knots. The construction palette alone makes the diagram material. Johnson clearly is a Modernist, designing

abstractly with light and space, but the Modernism is experientially enriched. The architect did not create an object but an environment that offers tactile experience as a foretaste of nature.

Back in Los Angeles, Johnson's own house is more introverted and internalized, its order determined by the tight organization of rooms on a small urban lot. Inside, Johnson denies the packing by opening rooms to each other, borrowing space within an open plan. The kitchen, living and dining areas flow into each other and onto an elevated courtyard, with a pool at the far end. Within the matrix of white walls, the architect nests exceptional moments, such as an elevated and sculptural blue-box fireplace overlooking the table in the dining room. He peels back the sheetrock strategically, to expose wood joists, for example, around a beam that passes above the wood dining table, itself split down the middle. The staircase, wide enough for occasional packs of children, erupts through the floors, one of the house's many "events" that cumulatively give the house a specific vertical character comparable to the unfolding horizontal character of the Napa house. Other exceptional pieces include a second cubic fireplace in the living room, suave black bookcases in the library, and a cylinder of frosted glass housing the study on the roof terrace. Each piece has a strong visual identity. Within the domestic landscape, Johnson turns the functional parts into markers in space. Johnson articulates the programmatic elements, giving them distinguishing forms, so that the whole becomes a well-tempered composite of purposely heterogeneous difference.

10

The notion of structure as architecture and urban design's basic organizing principle pervaded the history of Modernism, and Johnson and Fain apply their conceptual approach—significant topical variation on underlying structure—with remarkable consistency, and validity, across scales. At a middle range, Johnson Fain uses the same approach in its highly sophisticated design for Central High School No.10 in Los Angeles. The school district, having neglected high school construction for two decades, has embarked on an ambitious, remedial school building program. For a tight urban site and mixed-use program near downtown, the architects have conceived a high school structured on an urban rather than suburban model. Built out to the edges of its large block, with a bridge connecting it to sports fields on another block, the structure rings its site like circling wagons, forming a large courtyard whose spatial concentration focuses the school inward, fostering a sense of community. At the edge of the ring, facing out, the public elements of this mixed-use project front the street, reinforcing the fabric of the surrounding residential community.

Central High No.10 takes the shape of an arcaded cloister, but instead of keeping programs with a public role landlocked inside the building, Johnson brings

Private Residence, St. Helena, California
(see Figures 1.1–1.7)

Private Residence, Los Angeles
(see Figures 3.1–3.6)

the programmatic functions to the interior edge of the ring: the cafeteria, amphitheater, music rooms, shop—anything with a potentially animating presence outside are organized around the edge of the courtyard. Activities can spill out onto the concrete plinth in outdoor loggias ringing the court: musicians might set up a quartet in the sun; shop students might finish a chair. Architecturally, Johnson has tried to express differences of program and scale so that the structure is highly differentiated. He creates a fine-grain texture within a larger concept, giving detail to the diagram. Contrary to the more industrialized model of education, where schools have occupied standardized buildings that emphasize conformity, Johnson cultivates

difference. The programmatic elements animate the public spaces like events; he expresses rather than represses individuality and variety within the community. He even uses the building as a didactic tool, exposing the anatomy of its mechanical parts. Air ducts and wiring are revealed rather than covered. Clerestory windows are operable, suggesting issues of climate related to energy conservation.

In their practice, Johnson oversees the design of architecture, with Fain directing urban design and planning, and they frequently reciprocate expertise in their collaborations. Johnson came to the Pereira practice after working in the New York office of Philip Johnson while Fain came to Pereira with a precocious

12

LAUSD Central High School #10, Los Angeles
(see Figures 1.8–1.14)

career as an urbanist. He worked in the New York City Lindsay administration's progressive urban design group and went on to practice with the Boston Redevelopment Authority, which virtually invented urban revival in the United States. Fain also later worked with HUD restructuring troubled new towns.

China recently has shown signs of replacing Germany and Japan as the client state hiring hundreds of international talents, and in 2000, Johnson Fain won an international competition to master plan the Beijing Central Business District, a neighborhood not far from Tiananmen Square. Nowhere is the increasingly topical opposition of locality and globalization more salient as an issue than in this millennial culture as China searches for its place in an irreversibly globalizing world.

If the International Style assumed constants across cultures that predisposed architecture to abstraction, Johnson Fain instead investigates the specificities of culture surrounding a commission—however, not to slap facile local symbols on the design, like a Postmodernist citation, but to build up a design in layered responses that echo the fundamental character of a place. For the architects venturing into China, variation on the structure of an International Style rationalist paradigm offered the possibility of a design recognizable to foreigners doing business here, yet compatible with the China that Beijing wants to become. From an urban design point of view, grounding the international in the specificities of Beijing represented an adaptation of architectural globalization to Chinese cultural space.

Form was not the dominant generator of Fain's urban plan for Beijing. "At this scale, the hard

architectural sketch alone doesn't suffice," says Fain. "We draw on research. We're not sentimentally involved with the past, but we go back to old maps. We're trying to find out how all the social, cultural and physical pieces fit." Fain's research in Chinese town planning yielded the message that when Genghis Kahn established Beijing as his capital in the 13th century, he employed the grid to lay out the city. This urban tradition, with the Forbidden City at its core, informed the way Fain accommodated some 100 million square feet of mixed-use buildings on a vast 4-square kilometer site already crossed by two major intersecting roadways. The project, with Fain acting as team leader and urban designer, absorbs existing buildings from the Stalinist era as it centers itself on a proposed 140-story tower, the tallest in the world. Designed by Johnson, the skyscraper would climax a crescendo of buildings within a gridded pattern of city blocks laced with outdoor green zones and waterways, and furnished with public spaces and cultural venues.

By the time Fain absorbs a wide range of considerations resulting from his research, he has left simplicity behind in favor of more comprehensive solutions verging on the complex. Fain's urban concept for Beijing, which bested six other designs in an international competition, proposes that eight roughly-square blocks of buildings surround the most intensively developed central block. Skirting this area at the perimeter, and interspersed throughout the plan, are residential and commercial buildings. Within the Chinese tradition of axially symmetrical planning, the architect overlays the grid with concentric urban rings that diminish in density and intensity toward

13

the edges. A series of green zones—promenades and parks with canals and ponds—ring the inner ring, connecting a chain of cultural nodes devoted to music, sports, and art. A dozen distinct districts take on the coloring of these cultural facilities.

Fain also layers the plan with activities and services in an effort to build up a self-reinforcing, mixed-use urbanism with all the characteristics of a city that has developed organically over time. Besides the road grid organized around the two main thoroughfares, Fain has proposed a new below grade mass-transit line along with at-grade transit routes. Pedestrian and bike paths confirm the major vehicular arteries and the green belts, which link the cultural buildings into a loose necklace. The architectural massing of the housing respects the traditional Chinese concern for maximum southern exposure; the designers enhance this primitive strategy for husbanding warmth with more advanced concepts in energy conservation and sustainability.

Fain does not interpret literally the nine-square ideal of a traditional plan, bounded by walls with gates set on axis, but instead deforms and adapts the ideal to the existing and adjacent infrastructure. Interconnected enough so that it coheres as a self-defined district, the plan at its edges knits seamlessly with the surrounding roadways of the larger city, avoiding self-isolation within a walled compound. Based on an incremental rather than tabula rasa approach, the scheme is integrationist, developed through a process of urbanistic, architectural and programmatic layering that produces urban detail within a coherent whole. Like Johnson working at an architectural

14

scale, Fain creates a fine-grain texture within a larger concept, giving detail to the basic diagram. He injects urban variety with cultural facilities, monuments, and parks in Beijing's Central Business District. Confirming Chinese culture and tradition as it acknowledges Beijing's emergence as a world city, the multivalent plan hybridizes the old and new Chinas, and welcomes the rest of the world on local terms. The design is an object lesson in the Darwinian adaptation of a culture through the modification of its physical environment. The plan remains Chinese even as it evolves Chinese urban culture. Fain allows China to do what it has always done, absorb cultural invasions and make them Chinese.

The grid was already old when Genghis Kahn imported it to China. The originality of Fain's interpretation is that he relaxes it, blurring the edges, creating exceptional moments within its matrix. The exceptions to the rule include the meandering bodies of water that Fain lets into the site, and the string of cultural facilities. Fain allows punctual moments to mark the fabric. The grain makes the huge project accessible, and supports the programmatic notion that a city is an orchestrated performance of many parts moving dependently and independently at different rhythms.

This is a new city that looks seasoned, one with multiple scales, mixed uses, and differentiated building types and public spaces. The layered complexity is a far cry from the campus that Pereira created at Irvine, and the plans that Modernist forebears such as Le Corbusier created in capitals like Chandigargh. Fain was weaving together the city as a fabric rather than designing disconnected object-monuments in an open field. The plan creates a loose armature for growth that is not over controlled, but remarkably flexible, and subject to interpretation within a highly volatile society predicated on rapid change. Without superposing rigidity, the plan posits an alternative to the sprawl typical of new urban growth in Chinese cities.

In Sacramento, the urban and architectural plans for a district of five city blocks with a complex of government buildings represented a completely different set of cultural issues for another capital city, but one that again yielded high local specificity

within the rationalist paradigm. The State of California hired Johnson Fain to design the Capitol Area East End in Sacramento, where the state wanted to consolidate many agencies otherwise dispersed throughout Sacramento while reinforcing the fabric of the city. The program called for new standards of environmental activism. Johnson, acting as team leader and principal building designer, worked with Fain as the urban designer.

Fain's concern that the East End respond to the symmetry of the stately and historic West End encouraged Johnson to develop a symmetric and axial

15

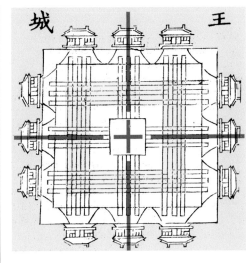

Beijing Central Business District, Beijing
(see Figures 2.1–2.9)

relationship between the new buildings and the Capitol. Together, they shared an interest in widening Capitol Avenue and introducing the qualities of Capitol Park into the heart of the new complex. At both architectural and urban scales, the design is systematic, each designer bringing exceptions into his system.

Often office buildings suffer from a monolithic character, and Johnson took care to break down the normal Euclidean solidity with changes of material and scale, corresponding to variations in the urban design. Johnson's design also translated to an architectural scale urban issues that migrated into the buildings through an open design process: the breakdown reflected findings in public hearings. Discussions with the community affected not only plans but also elevations, as the facades became a literal interface performing a transition between the government and the surrounding neighborhoods—between the architectural present and the historic past.

The degree of Johnson Fain's sensitivity to the social and intellectual contours of a commission is especially productive in their design of the Native American Museum and Cultural Center in Oklahoma. In their search for the essential character of the client and the basis for the discourse of their building, the architects plunged into research to comprehend Indian life. Fain, acting as team leader, emerged with an understanding based in its three formative ecologies—the plains, woodlands and rivers. The architects came to understand that all Indians share the notion of fire as the organizational center of their encampments and the fundamental source of energy. In this elemental world, the earth and sky

16

are spiritual, and recurrent events circle an axis of time.

The architects were searching for meaning within an environmental and cultural context rather than importing meaning to the site via a self-contained architectural language. The gestation of the project in the architects' imagination was conceptual rather than formal, and the central idea the architects evolved was to cultivate a seamless relationship between the earth and the building. The design calls for sheltering roofs that seem to grow out of an earth mound spiraling up from the plain. The architects ordered an entry sequence that starts in the earth, passing moments of water and fire, and climbs up to roof level as though approaching the sky. The promenade recalls the classic Indian spiritual progression from the earth to heaven. The building acts as the analogue of a spiritual path to transcendence.

At a time when the leveling forces of globalization are confirming the homogenizing rapacities of international architecture, Johnson and Fain emerge as culturalists trying to understand projects from within the genius loci. They are not simply parachuting into Oklahoma as aesthetic colonialists bearing a superior message, but are acting as interpreters developing the architectural and urban interface between the cultures converging on a design. They are relativists who understand that the intersection of outside and inside forces generates the meaning of each project.

One of the architects' common goals, whether at an architectural or urban scale, has been to organize and design buildings and city plans that cultivate urban life in a shaped public sphere. At Irvine, Fain achieved the goal with his pedestrian street, while

Johnson created a sense of community by urbanizing institutional buildings through the use of arcades, enclosed gardens and expressed circulation elements. Johnson has worked with private developers at a scale large enough that even commercial buildings have a strong public component.

The firm's strategy of taking an ordering concept as a point of departure for significant variation amounts to a form of design incrementalism: the architects add and subtract to and from a given. The approach is equally valid for a new design as for operations on a fact already on the ground.

Fain's concern for incremental urban development is perhaps best exemplified in a proposal for Los Angeles, exhibited in an urban design show at the Los Angeles Museum of Contemporary Art. The scheme is ingeniously opportunistic and simple: the architect advocated greening vestigial transportation medians, cemented riverbeds, and power line rights-of-way, and other underutilized belts. Fain was turning leftover spaces into outdoor recreation zones reminiscent of the "emerald necklace" designed by Frederick Law Olmsted throughout Boston. Fain's research revealed that Los Angeles, a city of backyards, seriously lacks

17

Oklahoma Native American Cultural Center & Museum, Oklahoma City (see Figures 1.15–1.20)

Capitol Area East End Complex, Sacramento, California (see Figures 2.10–2.17)

public outdoor space, despite its increasing densification by immigrant populations with a predisposition for an outdoor civic life. The green zones have an obvious usefulness in their immediate neighborhoods, but they also layer the city in circuits of greenery that establish connections between communities whose relationships have been severed by freeways and high-speed roadways. (Fain later imported this concept of green beltways to the project for Beijing's Central Business District).

For a redesign of Downtown Los Angeles's Civic Center, Fain took a radical, non-physical approach, designing by incremental programming. The Civic

Center has long been a lackluster urban underperformer, the buildings all belonging to separate branches of government isolated from one another by streets and a wide, landscaped mall. To animate the streetscape, Fain decided to extrovert the buildings by bringing program out of the building, populating the edges of the buildings and precincts with day care centers, cafeterias and conference rooms (much as the architects would do later, in the nearby Central High School No. 10). Fain was proposing to open, architecturally and bureaucratically, institutions closed to each other and to the street simply by deploying public amenities that already exist within the buildings.

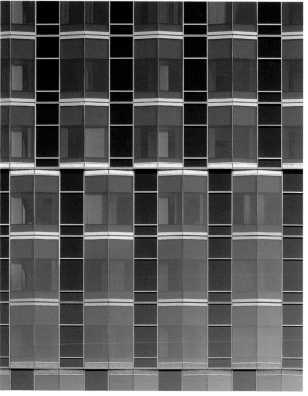

Los Angeles Open Space: A Greenways Plan, Los Angeles
(see Figures 6.1–6.7)

Constellation Place, Century City, California
(see Figures 6.19–6.23

Government, thought Fain, could be more accessible through a strategic reallocation of indoor facilities outside. The architect who does not necessarily visualize the city through sketches conceptualizes it instead in terms of urban animation. Unlike his predecessor, William Pereira, Fain derives urban form as a consequence and does not use it abstractly as a generator.

As architects in a generation that necessarily questioned Modernism, Johnson and Fain have succeeded in developing their own voice, embracing strategies of layering that encourage multiple readings. These reconstructed Modernists resist buildings and city plans that are too easy, structures and urban vistas that might impress the eye right away, but not inspire visitors to process their feelings about a building or city, on multiple visits remembered over time.

Both Johnson and Fain lived and worked through the upheavals in design over the last 25 years, and they have emerged able to move freely in and out of ideological camps. They would drive a Postmodernist axis through a plan, or monumentalize a building to take control of the surrounding space, if the design solution warranted those approaches. But their interest in the social implications and historic roots of design strategies, even those as obvious as the grid, have given their projects a larger cultural dimension that escapes stylistic labels.

The abstraction of their work, which may at first seem style based, is philosophically intentional, as it allows what Johnson calls "different avenues of entry"—the complexities and ambiguities whose polyvalence invites shifting interpretation. The architects do not try to control the responses of their visitors by aesthetic domination, but create instead suggestive environments that trigger multiple readings. The designs cohere, but loosely: they are not over structured. The architects isolate parts within loose conceptual and compositional wholes that allow multiple paths of understanding. Visitors complete the buildings and plans in their own experience and perception.

For Johnson Fain, design is not linear and pat. Rather than strain for the closure of perfection, the architects leave room for the unexpected, even the irrational. Whether in Napa or Beijing or Los Angeles, the architects cultivate lateral thinking, the exceptional events that give life—and pause—to a structure that tends to the ideal. Johnson believes that design, to achieve power, must engage the shadowy corners of the psyche, the locus of Freud's id, he says, and Jacques Derrida's joker, where beauty is radicalized and surprising.

After all the research, it is the leap into the unpredictable and unforeseeable that most interests Johnson Fain.

19

the LITERAL, the ABSTRACT, and a case for DEEP STRUCTURE

SCOTT JOHNSON I'd like to begin with a conversation on the impact of global communications on urban space and the radical decentralization that comes with it. Of course, global markets promote global communications, which tend to marginalize written language. Whether surfing an international web site, or buying things on the Net, regional language or place-specific references are increasingly excised. While English is the fallback language on the Net, the visuals, the formatting, instruction sequences, and the icons are the real operative language. We exist in a visual marketplace.

BILL FAIN The question is how do global communications in the Information Age affect the definition of urban space—the way we perceive the spatial sequences within the city. As in the past, just as the car and telephone have allowed the decentralization of the city, so the computer and the Net, are further helping to decentralize our cities. The language of space is changing. This trend will reinforce the notion of the regional city and the exurban city, one that does not rely on a traditional town square. Decentralization brings with it a set of conflicts or dualities: regionalism vs. internationalism, the finite vs. the infinite, local vs. universal.

As cultures change because of the Information Age, issues arise concerning historic preservation and regional identity. As designers engaged with projects in China and Europe, we struggle with this because we look to the locality and its history in search of content for the project that will distinguish it from other projects and cities. If the Internet offers up the same info all over the world, it is bound to introduce sameness much in the way our suburbs have the same Taco Bells and McDonalds, anywhere USA. Differences should be celebrated in the Information Age, but the forces are there which will create sameness. These are big questions that face cities, and as designers I am not sure we have much control over them, but they must be considered.

PRIVATE RESIDENCE | ST. HELENA, CALIF. | 1994 | FIGURES 1.1–1.7

1.1 A five-bedroom vacation home in Napa Valley is designed to maximize views and local site conditions and offer a highly structured yet informal living experience.

PRIVATE RESIDENCE | ST. HELENA, CALIF. | 1994 | 1.2

SJ It seems to me that one of the ways to view many of our design activities within the office is to think of a term used in the study of linguistics, that is, deep structure. There was, in the days of Noam Chomsky (a professor at MIT during our time at Harvard), the idea that the structure of communication revolved around basic conceptual forms and recurring essential urges. There was thought to be, in effect, a deep structure that was at the heart of possibly infinite linguistic variations. It is common here in the office, when we are beginning to design something, to hover about, to research, to visit, to look at history, to examine what we might consider comparables in some explicit or subtle way.

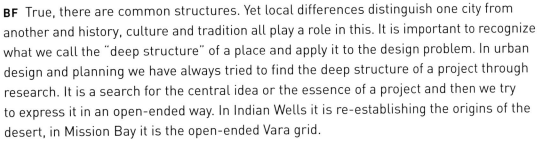

Noam Chomsky

This is an acknowledgement of intuitive forces that exist in our understanding of the design mission we are about to undertake. We are asking ourselves what exists before we arrive, and how, and for what purpose are we intending to intervene? This identification of deep structure is frequently a "mending" of sorts. Of seeing whatever pattern preceded our activities, and then designing missing links which either complete a broken sequence or suggest a new vector, a transformation to an unfolding reality. This way of approaching the design is applicable, I believe, whether we are working on Amgen in Southern California, on a winery in Northern California, or in the Central Business District of Beijing, China.

BF True, there are common structures. Yet local differences distinguish one city from another and history, culture and tradition all play a role in this. It is important to recognize what we call the "deep structure" of a place and apply it to the design problem. In urban design and planning we have always tried to find the deep structure of a project through research. It is a search for the central idea or the essence of a project and then we try to express it in an open-ended way. In Indian Wells it is re-establishing the origins of the desert, in Mission Bay it is the open-ended Vara grid.

Often resulting from our research in both urban design and architecture, right or wrong, we will "center" things. This helps to create a clearly identifiable "place." And we try to understand this place within its context by drawing upon the city's history. We try to understand what the region or the locality is all about. The use of history is not about

1.2 Johnson protected the interior from the nearby road by creating a double line-up of closed cubes whose backs face the street: each cube contains a room.

1.3 Starting with the compressed entrance and ending with the release into the view, the house delivers the family to the out of doors through the vector of its interior space.

PRIVATE RESIDENCE │ ST. HELENA, CALIF. │ 1994 │ 1.3

1.4 The informal formality achieves warmth through a material palette that includes concrete block, smooth flagstone, slate tiles, plywood paneling, hand applied white-gold leaf, and exposed wood joists.

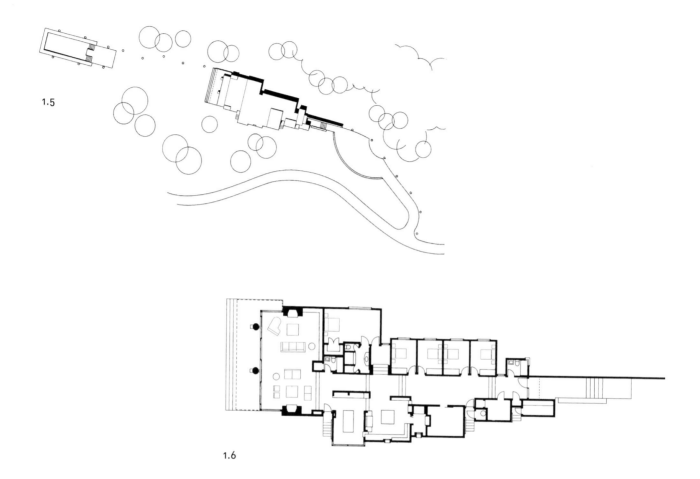

1.5

1.6

1.5, 1.6 An axial promenade
from the front door continues
straight through the line-up
of rooms. The blinded hallway
steps down the slope to a
spacious, glass-lined living
room that opens onto an
expansive terrace facing the
sweeping view.

being sentimental but rather it is used to inform us about the past to better understand the future. The use of history is not about a nostalgic attachment to traditional forms and images.

SJ But it is very hard to do that, very hard to comprehend a particular place without getting tangled up in the collective sentiment, the self-image or identity of a region. Attempts to identify the deep structure of a place can help us to bypass these issues, but a huge range of artists from Warhol, down to Cindy Sherman and Jeff Koons, as well as a host of Postmodern critics and semioticians, have tried to convince us that a thing is, in effect, a sign, and, as such, its meaning equates to the response it evokes. Talk about feeding the drive to be popular! This is a strange and potentially lethal mix of semiotics, sentimentality and globalized architecture. One need only look at the imagery of shopping centers, resorts and most of the New Urbanism to know that calculated and collective sentimentality is a living force in our culture. We know that sphere of culture is out there, but other things interest us more.

Andy Warhol, *Telephone*, 1961

BF In fairness, preoccupation with the universal has its pitfalls, too. We have learned from the first generation of modern architecture that the importation of an "international" idea into a local setting can be jarring, to say the least. The social and cultural adaptation to Brasilia, despite being in existence for many years, is still taking place. Modernism often challenges local culture, its spatial continuity, and the traditional function of places. In the past, there has been a kind of disconnect or detachment between the "universal" idea of modern architecture and urban design and local human habitats. What I mean by detachment is that modernism often lacks scale and hierarchy, and is hard to relate to, in a local cultural sense.

Brasilia

SJ The first time around, European modernism worked to avoid the symbols that were culturally specific. This time around, and in the wake of an extended post-modern, post-structuralist critique, the best modernism seems

30

1.7 The 5-bedroom program also offers small spatial opportunities and casual moments.

to be highly layered, and can embrace overlapping realities, the either/and, in this case, the universal and the specific.

BF So we've learned from the first generation of modernism that it has many shortcomings. There are whole movements today that consider re-creating the past as better than creating something new for the future. We support the "New Urbanist" doctrine which relates design to local conditions and to a more "human scale," but we do not subscribe to its frequent disregard of our contemporary culture and literal translation of the past into the future. That's not acceptable as far as I am concerned.

SJ The past is a hard place to be in the present.

31

BF It's an easy place to be, because you can literally copy. It's harder to invent something new.

SJ Yes, easy for construction, but hard for architecture. The problem is that so much of our cultural output—fine arts, music, cinema, graphics, and so on—has become so mechanistic and the global marketplace, as we have been discussing, tends to reduce all things to signs. In architectural terms, a "style" is, in effect, a sign. There is a presumed universe of forms, or moves, which are identifiably within the realm of the sign. So, it should come as no surprise that a significant amount of current architectural work we would now call Modern is not actually contemporary, or new, but rather, semiotic, or historicist in the sense that the sign has been acknowledged broadly, and now draws meaning from its own recognition. It's like being famous for being famous.

My own belief is that, in architecture, a search for deep structure and a concern for abstraction are almost always useful devices. They establish a more open, or to use an old Charles Jencks term, a more multivalent portal that is accessible to more people. If you design something that is totally narrative or regionally literal, received meaning is limited to a pre-screened, culturally specific group of users. This is a kind of prescriptive and monolithic form of communication between sender and receiver that bodes badly for the world of invention.

1.8 Central Los Angeles High School No. 10 is designed around a landscaped academic quadrangle and a public "town square" giving access to student services, cafeteria and assembly spaces. Located on twenty acres at the edge of downtown Los Angeles, the school complex accommodates 1,700 students. In order to serve a number of area high schools, the program includes a special emphasis on sports facilities, that include two large gymnasia and an Olympic swimming pool.

LAUSD CENTRAL HIGH SCHOOL #10 | LOS ANGELES | 2001 | FIGURES 1.8–1.14

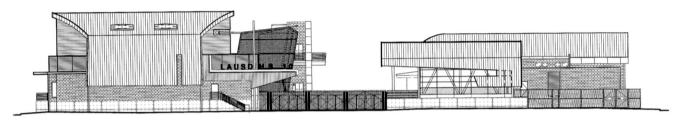

1.9

1.10

1.9 Entry elevation
1.10 Side elevation

LAUSD CENTRAL HIGH SCHOOL #10 │ LOS ANGELES │ 2001 │ 1.9, 1.10

BF Yet, in most of what is created in cities today, the literal prevails. I believe abstraction in design is by far the more interesting particularly with regard to artistic composition. There is a universal quality to it. It leaves room for imagination and interpretation and something to reach for from the observer that is artistically interesting. But for the average guy, it is more comfortable and easier to understand a literal architectural expression of the past. That is why most of our society seems to gravitate to the literal— that's why Disney World and all those places are so popular.

SJ They are products of formula.

BF They are cartoon interpretations of history. You go to Las Vegas and see the Luxor pyramid, and 95 percent of the population does not realize that the pyramids are outside Cairo, not in Luxor.

SJ Luxor is just a more suggestive and identifiable name. A better brand, if you will....

BF ...which doesn't even really matter. So, it's easier and more accessible, this kind of literal visual language.

SJ I'm not sure if we agree on this topic.

The Luxor, Las Vegas

BF Let me come, at this point, from a slightly different angle. I believe that we often enter our profession because of our personal desire to create or need to be artistic. Through our education we come to understand another set of needs, which are to serve society and/or solve the problems of a client. These artistic needs have to do with personal choices regarding composition, and abstract thinking and expression is a part of this. These needs sometimes run counter to the needs to provide service that is some-thing that literally addresses a local problem. Our work can be described as a delicate balance or the creative tension that exists between this internal artistic need and that external service need.

1.12 View of the Media Center

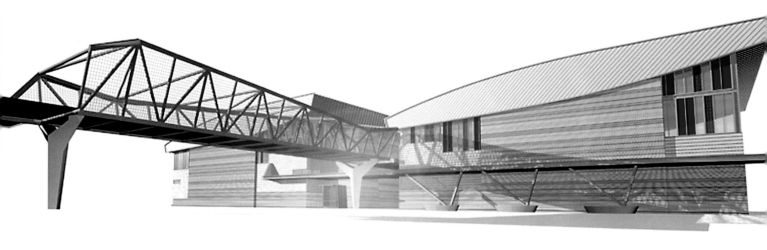

SJ I agree with Bill's observation of the facts, although I believe there are other facts that both support and deny his position. First, my comments on abstraction refer to a more multi-dimensional engagement with content than solely with "compositional elements." Still, he is right to identify its opposite as literalism, which is of course a consensual fabrication of a presumed reality.

Perhaps a good part of our difference here has to do with what we earlier described as our relative design missions, in this case, urban design and architecture. It is my observation that Bill and the urban design studio here are generally engaged in an explicitly "macro" process, one that involves a wide range of stakeholders, is frequently community based, and is likely to be considered inter-generational, that is, the work is a bridge between what went before, and what comes after.

In architecture, and even in works of scale, the design process is frequently more focused. There is a sense that the stakeholders are knowable, and not infinite. And importantly, there is a figure/ground relationship between architecture and planning. In architecture, we may choose to radicalize our context in some meaningful way. We may determine, after consideration, that a strategic aberration to the planning zeitgeist may add value and reinforcement to both the work of architecture and the planning framework. At the very least, we know, or think we know, that the work will be built and it will establish a little microcosm of infinite and implied physical relations. In this, abstraction seems a necessary tool. Still, we hope to remain accessible.

BF True, in urban design and planning, projects are seen as a part of a continuum, that is, there is a past en route to the future—this occurs in part because of the stakeholders that Scott mentions and possibly because of the large scale of intervention that normally accompanies urban design projects. But, I disagree with Scott about the term "macro"— I would like to call it "conceptual". We do look for the "big idea" in urban design and planning and it often resides in the concept. This is not to say we are not focused. Many of our projects become Specific Plans such as the Indian Wells landscape corridor, urban design guidelines at Mission Bay, and even architecture as in the cases of the Native American Cultural Center and the Piers projects. Furthermore, I would like to suggest that the figure/ground relationship between architecture and planning does exist in urban design, which is exactly what we do. This is a physical design office and we are not process planners.

39

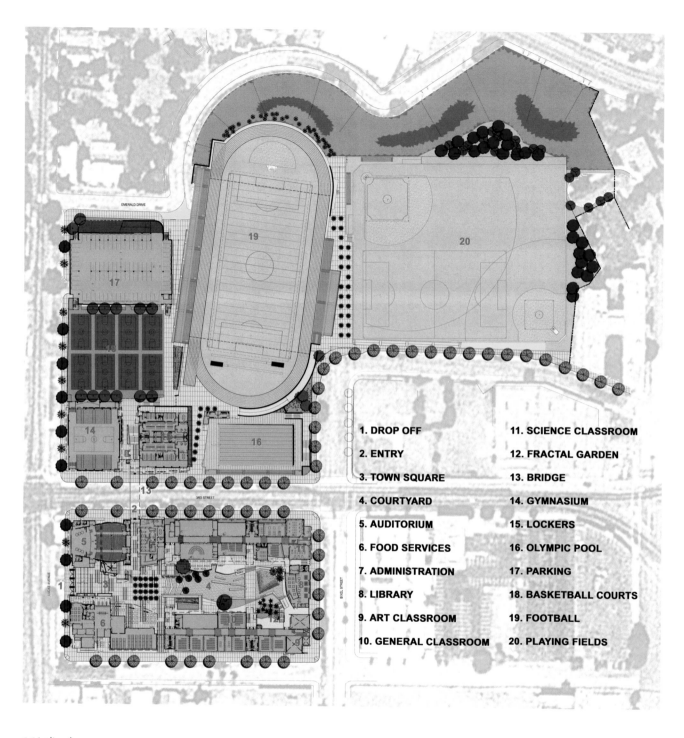

1. DROP OFF
2. ENTRY
3. TOWN SQUARE
4. COURTYARD
5. AUDITORIUM
6. FOOD SERVICES
7. ADMINISTRATION
8. LIBRARY
9. ART CLASSROOM
10. GENERAL CLASSROOM
11. SCIENCE CLASSROOM
12. FRACTAL GARDEN
13. BRIDGE
14. GYMNASIUM
15. LOCKERS
16. OLYMPIC POOL
17. PARKING
18. BASKETBALL COURTS
19. FOOTBALL
20. PLAYING FIELDS

1.14 site plan

I would like to comment on another point made. It is impossible to do urban design and planning under an "infinite" stakeholder condition. In most cases, we try to establish the limits to the stakeholder condition, allowing us to understand the degree of predictability. It is my observation that in our office a similar condition exists in architecture. This is normal, given the complex urban problems faced daily by most projects in our office.

The issue of accessibility is where Scott and I have disagreement. What Scott is trying to get at is that there are certain qualities about abstraction that are universal, that have to do with proportion, with the way that light enters buildings...

SJ ...and more. On the physical level, where we experience a building directly, there is procession, the elaboration of an envelope, orientations, transparencies, time. On the linguistic level we have discussed, where architecture is semiotic, and functions as information, there is the relation of the work to other typologies, the embrace or denial of common functional assumptions, or the reinterpretation of semantic elements in the work, say, doors, windows, walls, whatever.

BF And moving from one culture to another, these elements are understood across quite a broad range of conditions. I think that most probably our disagreement is to the degree these are accessible, and universally understood and appreciated from one culture to another.

I would like to refer to the Japanese and their early villas—Kinkaku-ju or Katsura and the site plan for Shugakuin Villa both in Kyoto—with views and orientations which are very subtle and extremely beautifully designed, organized to express an idea about the universe, of the infinite vs. the finite. The rooms at Katsura are arranged so there is no need for the traditional "western" hallway. Spaces and the transitions between them are related to the garden. The walls are moveable screens, which are translucent and divide the garden from the space indoors. The use of natural elements like stone and water is a part of the overall composition. Although the villas were built in the 17th century, elements seem contemporary, abstract, and most people understand them today. We feel very comfortable in these buildings, because they seem like something

1.15 The story of the 39 federally recognized tribes of Oklahoma goes back to the Relocation Act of 1830, when there was a forced relocation of Indian tribes from various parts of the United States to Oklahoma—this was the famous "Trail of Tears." The site is 330 acres located on the North Canadian River across from downtown Oklahoma City. The gestation of the project was conceptual rather than formal, and the central idea was to cultivate a seamless relationship between the earth and the building.

OKLAHOMA NATIVE AMERICAN CULTURAL CENTER & MUSEUM | OKLAHOMA CITY, OKLAHOMA | 1999 | FIGURES

1.16 Within the 300 acres are the three ecologies, which represent the original native habitats of the 39 tribes—the plains, the river, and the woodlands. All Indians share the notion of fire as the organizational center of their encampments and the fundamental source of energy. An entry sequence starts in the earth, passing moments of water and fire, and climbs up to roof level as though approaching the sky.

that we might have built in the last 30 years here. There is a universal, timeless quality that is quite amazing. At the same time, they are local.

SJ They are local and they are not. They are different and the same.

BF The villas were created by a very sophisticated culture at the time, and probably the average person did not have access to them.

SJ Of course. Japanese gardens were a great inspiration to many of the early modernist architects. They sensed their meaning, even if they did not fully understand the gardens in their own culturally specific terms. You are right that in the end there are things about the garden and its culture that you won't understand unless you're Japanese, or perhaps you've read Marc Treib or Charles Moore on the topic. Having said that, you know what rock is; you know what raked gravel does. You know how maples transform light, and you may have physical responses to pruned azaleas and bound bamboo. And you probably sense the implied infinity of the garden. These are things that are fundamental to our experience which we identified earlier as the elements of deep structure. I think these designs are highly accessible, even if you haven't read the book and you haven't made all the cultural connections. Your first broken pediment may mean nothing to you, but when you see a huge rock placed next to a perfectly hewn timber, you can at least get some-where with that.

BF The Japanese work, particularly at the Shugakuin Villa, challenges Western ideas of procession—the way we approach a place—illusion, and our perception of wholeness. For instance, at the Shugakuin Villa in Kyoto, you enter into the garden along a very tight, constrained pathway that takes you to the villa. As you approach, you are unable to see the overall size and shape of the villa and its grounds—at first you do not even see it. You come around to the corner between two hedges, and find yourself going up some steps, and ahead of you is a room that is totally open to the outdoors. You walk beneath maple trees and in the room you see the shadow of maple leaves on the far wall, outlined by the

45

1.17 In the building are a series of experiences that inform you about Native American history, which in most cases is quite different than the history of the white man. There is also a Hall of Honor where digitized screens teach you about significant elders.

1.18 The design calls for sheltering roofs that seem to grow out of an earth mound spiraling up from the plain. The promenade recalls the classic Indian spiritual progression from the earth to heaven. The building acts as the analogue of a spiritual path to transcendence.

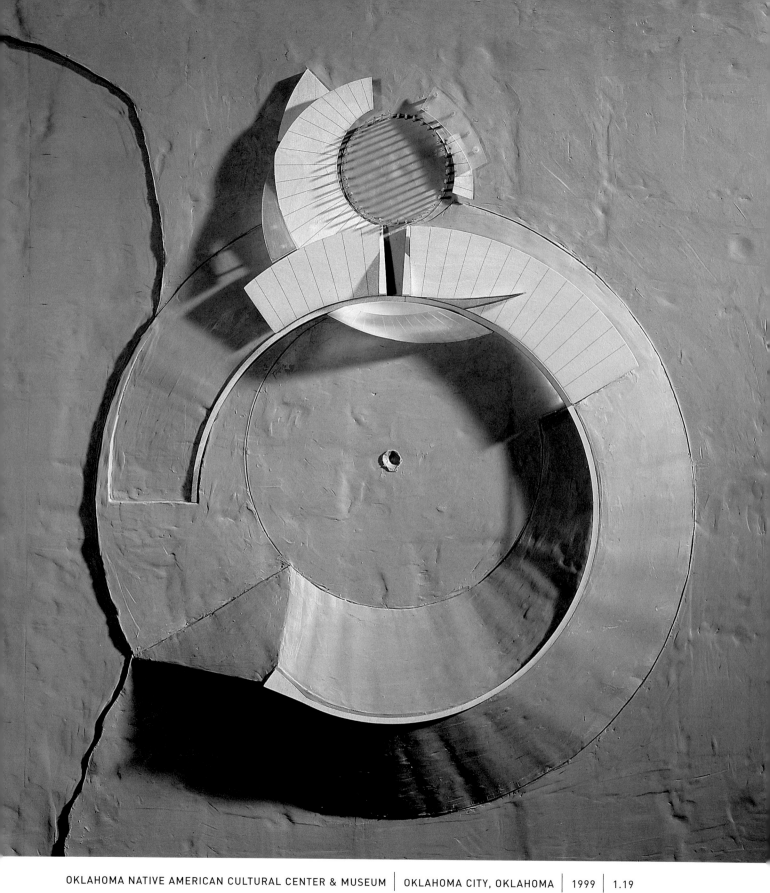

sunlight. As you approach, you realize that it is a cloudy day and there is no direct sun-light. It is an illusion. The shadow of the maple leaves is stenciled on the wall in gold leaf. The leaves are rendered in a literal way, but the illusion is an abstract concept.

You continue to move around the villa but have no sense of how large the villa is. You can enter, but stay outside and continue into the garden. Continuing along, you walk down towards a lake, there is an island pavilion—a small "folly". You near the water's edge and walk around a bend that turns back in the direction of the villa. Here, you can look back across the lake and for the first time you can see the entire garden, lake, and villa, and you realize how large a complex this place is. You have progressed through a series of small episodes, each building an impression of this wonderful place yet none summarizing the whole place for you, until the end of the procession, when you are able to view the entire garden and villa.

49

In contrast, the Western approach is much more direct. Views of an entire estate are seen upfront—the whole thing. You drive through a gate, look across a green and there's the edifice. The view happens upfront, where as in the east, you evolve towards the view at the end. As Westerners, we put ourselves at the middle of the universe, while in the east, they back themselves into it.

SJ You never perceive the edges of a Japanese garden environment, because the edges are not imagined to exist. The Japanese garden is a paradigm of the universe. It's a poetic, scenographic thing, much as the scholar, Gaston Bachelard, described designed objects and physical space. Landscape as miniature, a garden microcosm of the universe. The Japanese are brilliant at conceiving it and playing it out.

What Bill is talking about is a way of conceiving and using abstraction, with a fairly high understanding of the way that garden works, and the intentions of the designers of that garden. Maybe an average visitor does not have all this intellectual context, but he can still have a full experience. When you talk about the Western dialectic of literalism and abstraction, and the danger of sentimentality, well, there is nothing sentimental about that garden.

BF The idea of a deep structure occurs again in our work with the Native American Center in Oklahoma City. As they have explained it to us, the Native American has a world

50

1.19 "The entrance to the Native American complex is a series of fragments or arcs. Native Americans believe that life is circular—it's actually a spiral that is like a circle progressing through time. You come upon the same experiences again and again in life, but then again they are not the same, because you have progressed. The center is defined by combining the building and earth."

1.20 "The earth and building are totally inseparable in design—the building is within the mound. You enter the earth, and visible through the glass windows of the Hall of the People is the eternal fire at the center of the circular mound— the encampment."

view that is episodic, where things tend to be seen as events. The idea of wholeness is within each event and is not necessarily a progression from A to B to C, as we might expect in Western thinking. The icons of Native American culture are very symbolic. It is not about religion as outsiders might know it. Their beliefs are about nature and living in nature. For example, they have a belief that man evolves from earth—not land, which in Western minds is a commodity—but earth,which is spiritual and then ascends to the heavens. As we have come to understand from the Oklahoma Indians, life is circular where events come upon themselves over and over again through a progression of time. This belief becomes the central idea or armature upon which the project is organized— its deep structure.

Our involvement with the Native American project began with a site selection study a number of years ago. The story of the 39 federally recognized tribes of Oklahoma goes back to the Relocation Act of 1830, when there was a forced relocation of Indian tribes from various parts of the United States to Oklahoma—this was the famous "Trail of Tears." To tell their story, the State of Oklahoma set up a special authority to build the Center and Oklahoma City donated the land. The site itself is 300 acres on the North Canadian River across from downtown Oklahoma City, at what is called the "crossroads of America", the intersection of I-35 and I-42. This site was the Number One oil-drilling site in Oklahoma and the land was totally depleted of its resources by the American settlers, between the 1880s and the 1950s. The land is interesting because it is within the flood plain and seemingly has no commercial value, and even has some "hot spots" of contamination. The Native Americans intend to return the land, the earth rather, to its original pristine condition.

SJ Some family relations never change, huh?

BF Well, there have been a number of events through history that have left the Indian in an increasingly worse condition, and these are stories that need to be told, and will be told quite interestingly in the content for the museum. We started out with the idea of settlement on the river, and how to characterize that in terms of the land form. We developed an idea of procession that starts in the earth and proceeds to the

| ST. ANDREW'S ABBEY | VALYERMO, CALIF. | 2003 | FIGURES 1.21–1.22 |

top of a mound, a spirit mound, symbolizing that man is born from the earth and ascends to heaven. The vertical axis is time and the procession is circular. You enter the project by experiencing the simple elements that were naturally a part of Native America—elements such as earth, wind, fire and water. As you approach the project, you proceed through a small forest. It is a hot day and you see a linear pond and feel cool mist from it. You enter a circular colonnade of pipes, one for each tribe, and you hear the sounds of the wind. The earth and building are totally inseparable in design—the building is within the mound. You enter the earth, and visible through the glass windows of the Hall of the People is the eternal fire at the center of the circular mound—the encampment.

Within the 300 acres are the three ecologies, which represent the original native habitats of the 39 tribes—the plains, the river, and the woodlands. In the building are a series of experiences that inform you about Native American history, which in most cases is quite different than the history of the "white man". There is also a Hall of Honor where digitized screens teach you about significant elders.

SJ We are talking again about the dialectic of abstraction and the literal, and how deep structure is the connecting link to a common human experience. This discussion persists throughout the office on a range of designs for religious, archaic, and, for lack of a better word, transcendental programs. Bill has described the cultural deep structure that forms the basis for the design of the Native American Center. Similar questions surround our redesign for All Saints Church in Beverly Hills as well as our current work on a Benedictine monastery in the desert, Saint Andrew's Abbey.

The monastery is in the desert, so the design has a lot to do with the specifics of desert form—the flora and fauna, the flatness and the quality of light—and in that sense, the building is regional. There are elements of iconography and symbolism that, pardon the phrase, form the story line, that is, the Benedictine story. And we know there have been nearly 2,000 years of Roman Catholic churches. Still we have no interest in doing something that has already been done, or is not specific to our own time and place. We wanted to enter a creative path, the end of which we could not identify. It's probably a good metaphor for designing any interesting building. In the church, as in any building, there is a program. The monks convene a processional, end up at the altar, and perform specific liturgical acts, and there is prayer, song, and some interaction with congregants.

53

1.21 "Saint Andrew's Abbey, a Benedictine monastery in the desert, is inspired by the flora and fauna, the flatness and the quality of light. We tried to create a solemnity in the space and impart a processional clarity to the liturgical elements. But we were not interested in imitating any iconography."

1.22 "The monks convene a processional, end up at the altar, and perform specific liturgical acts—there is prayer, song, and some interaction with congregants. The design creates a sense of place, of the quietude and humility of the Benedictine order that occupies it."

But again, we tried to unburden it, to strip it to the essentials, and focus on each act. We tried to create a sense of place, with a sense of the uniqueness of this extraordinary desert environment where nothing is superfluous, and a sense of the quietude and humility of the Benedictine order that occupies it. We tried to create a solemnity in the space and impart a processional clarity to the liturgical elements. But we were not interested in imitating any iconography. I think this is a common challenge.

BF The iconography is just the cross and the altar. At All Saints, it's a little different, because the attempt there was to clarify the structure.

SJ That was an existing building that we significantly remodeled.

55

BF You might mention the acoustics, the sound of the choir. The intent was to enable the music to resonate through the space.

SJ In that sense, All Saints is itself a musical instrument. It was originally designed and built as a traditional, processional Christian church and the nave, like any large longitudinal nave, has a resonant term, an interval, that has to be supported acoustically so that spoken word can be understood and religious music can also be appreciated in the style in which it was written. The monastery was a little different, because the monks traditionally sing by themselves, and only on occasion sing with a congregation. There is an important distinction to be made between activities of the monks and the congregation, when there is one. Basically, the monastery is both a reclusive site in which the monks honor their vows and a pilgrimage site.

All these projects deal explicitly with abstraction because the building, in each case, is at best a frail wrapper for an historic and ritual experience. We try to focus our efforts at a conceptual level, really, an essential level. You learn what is essential in a place, and what you can reduce it to.

All Saints Parish, Beverly Hills

SANDY LANE GOLF CLUBHOUSE | BARBADOS | 2002 | FIGURES 1.23–1.25

SANDY LANE GOLF CLUBHOUSE │ BARBADOS │ 2002 │ 1.24

SANDY LANE GOLF CLUBHOUSE | BARBADOS | 2002 | 1.25

SUSTAINABILITY
NATURE and TRADITION

BF Building orientation for solar access is a big factor in our China work. This is particularly evident in the large scale urban design projects—the designs for the Central Business District in Beijing and the Jiangwan Sub-town Center in Shanghai are major additions to their cities and currently under construction. Open spaces, parks and roads are oriented in ways that give buildings direct sunlight for a minimum of two hours each day. This is a planning regulation throughout China. You can see it in the east-west oriented "bar-like" buildings of the Maoist period. I am sure this policy was adopted partly because China has not had the energy to heat buildings. Scott, remember the winter meetings we've had in Beijing, where temperatures inside are freezing and we all have to wear overcoats and caps to stay warm?

Orienting buildings for solar access and building orientation goes back a thousand years. Neighborhoods in Beijing were developed in large blocks, with lots of small walking streets connected to courtyards surrounded by one and two-story homes. Buildings were built together and spaces are well defined— this aggregation was called *hutong*. A similar, more recent type of development in Shanghai is the *lelong*. Unfortunately, during the Maoist period, the Chinese did not fully learn from earlier models—on the one hand, learning about the need for solar access but, on the other hand, totally disregarding socio-spatial forms of courtyard and walking street. When you look at communities planned and buildings built from the 50s, you will see there is a strong linear dimension to site planning with the bar-like buildings dominating with no regard for arranging the buildings around a courtyard, like the traditional hutongs once did. The modern cities look very undefined because of that—spaces lack clarity and definition. A universal notion of solar access has been executed with total disregard for local tradition.

Hutong, Beijing

62

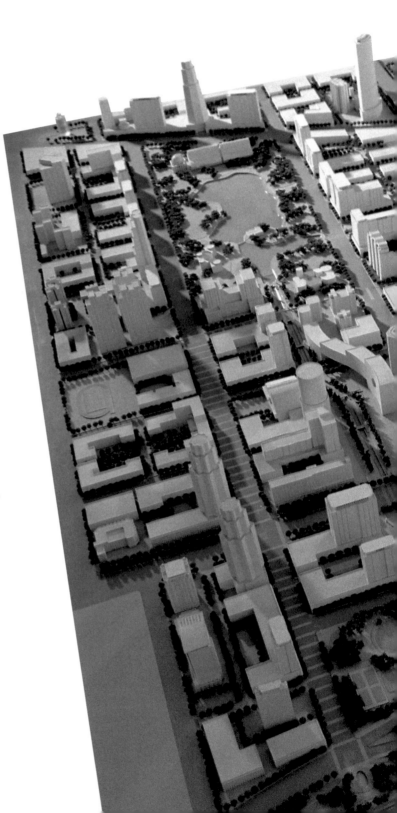

2.1 Johnson Fain's plan for a four-square km section of Beijing east of Tiananmen Square creates the city's first Central Business District. The project provides more than 100 million square feet of mixed–use development, including office, residential, retail, a wide range of cultural uses and more than 500 different buildings anchored by a central "City within a City," featuring a landmark 140-story tower. The Central Business District is composed of multiple unique neighborhoods linked by physical adjacency, multiple transit options, distinct street grids for pedestrians and vehicles, and a major parks network containing a "necklace" of premier cultural institutions. Mid-block walkways based on the traditional hutong are encouraged for small-scale pedestrian movement. Among proposed building regulations are standards to provide solar access for structures and public spaces.

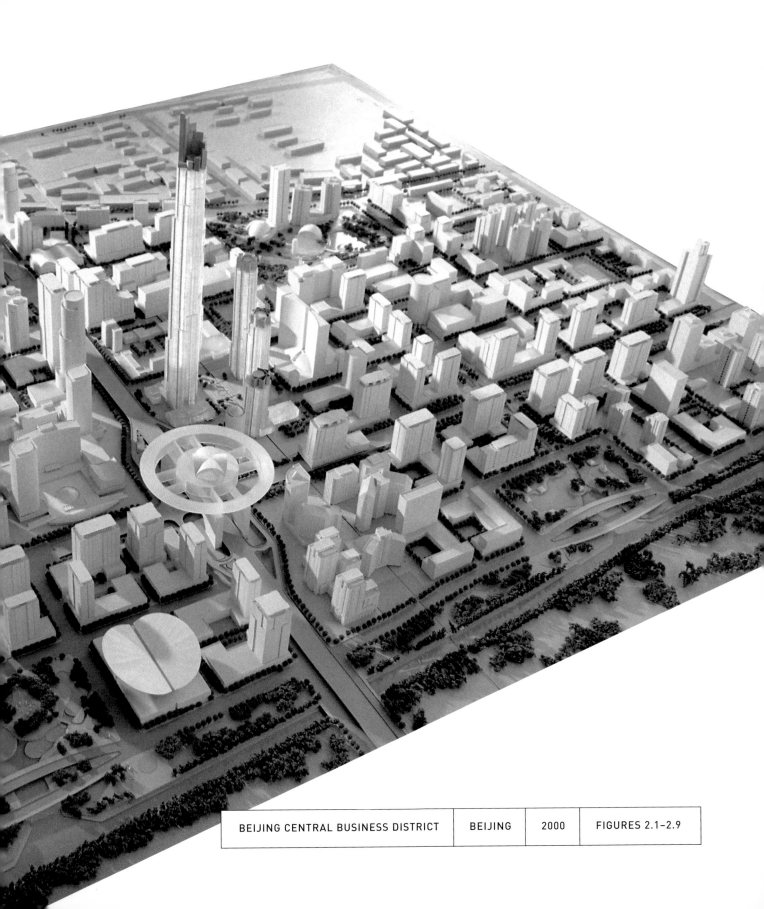

| BEIJING CENTRAL BUSINESS DISTRICT | BEIJING | 2000 | FIGURES 2.1–2.9 |

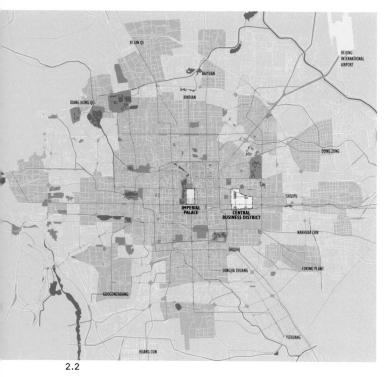

2.2

2.3

2.2 Historically, neighborhoods in Beijing were developed in large blocks with lots of small walking streets connected to courtyards surrounded by one and two-story homes. Buildings were built together and spaces are well defined in what was called "hutong".

2.3 "The hutong tradition is a beautiful example of how a design solution can be culturally specific without being sentimental or nostalgic, of the possibility of telling an old story that is still germane today. Our lives are different in so many ways now but this goal, and possibly this historically rooted pattern, of solar orientation might remain constant."

SJ The hutong tradition is a beautiful example of how a design solution can be culturally specific without being sentimental or nostalgic, of the possibility of telling an old story that is still germane today. Our lives are different in so many ways now but this goal, and possibly this historically rooted pattern, of solar orientation might remain constant. This is the kind of trace element I would identify as "deep structure". As it happens, it is also culturally specific. Much of the pre-Modern design and construction throughout Asia refer to archaic rituals that have survived over time and are *de facto* historically sustainable. The more recent marriage in these cultures of the drive to be modern, and the global accumulation of large investment capital has created instant patterns that may not be sustainable over the mid- or long-term.

65

BF In the earlier examples, the intent is to air-condition and heat buildings by use of building orientation. Solar orientation is required by law in China today, but with the new mechanics of buildings now underway they may soon reconsider this—just like in America where urban development has little regard for these issues. Let's be fair about it, only in recent years there has been a chorus of professionals and environmental activists supporting policies like LEED certification in building design. Hopefully they will be even more comprehensively applied in the future.

SJ In a similar way, some of the European standards in office design are way ahead of us in the way they mandate shallower building depths and natural light at the core of the building. Throughout Western Europe we are beginning to see multiple skins on the exterior of buildings that provide complex insulation and sun control while preserving visibility. We have also seen the use of large-scale heat sinks, high-rise gardens, and an emphasis on fresh air and indoor air quality. In the States, we are frequently confronted with fixed budgets that did not contemplate holistic sustainability, so we look toward technology and new products to achieve these goals. It's regrettably a more two-dimensional approach.

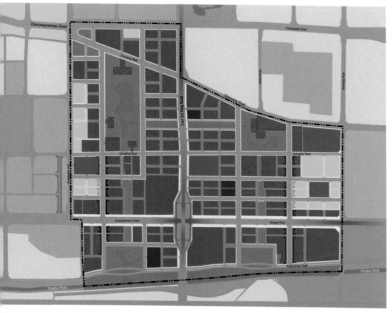

2.4

2.5

有拱廊的街道 ——————— ARCADES

商店街 ——————— RETAIL STREETS

穿越街廊的行人街道 ——————— MID-BLOCK PEDESTRIAN STR

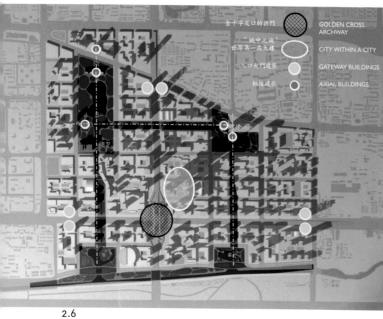

2.6

金十字交口的拱門 ● GOLDEN CROSS ARCHWAY

"城中之城" ⬭ CITY WITHIN A CITY
世界第一高大樓

入口大門建築 ◯ GATEWAY BUILDINGS

軸線建築 ◯ AXIAL BUILDINGS

2.7

•••••••• CULTURAL NE

1. SPORTS ARENA
2. SPORTS CLUB A
   MUSEUM
3. GOVERNMENT
   CENTER
4. MUSEUM OF CH
   TEXTILES & HAN
5. PUBLIC LIBRARY
6. RESTAURANT O
   LAKE
7. IMAX THEATER
   MUSEUM OF SC
   INDUSTRY
8. MUSEUM OF
   TRANSPORTATIC
9. PERFORMING AR
10. MUSEUM OF NA
    HISTORY
11. METROPOLITAN
    OF ART
12. MUSEUM OF MC
13. CHINESE MUSEL
    CERAMICS & SCI
    MUSEUM AND C
14. BEIJING THEATE
    CENTER
15. NATIONAL WAX
16. MUSEUM OF MII
17. CHILDREN'S ML

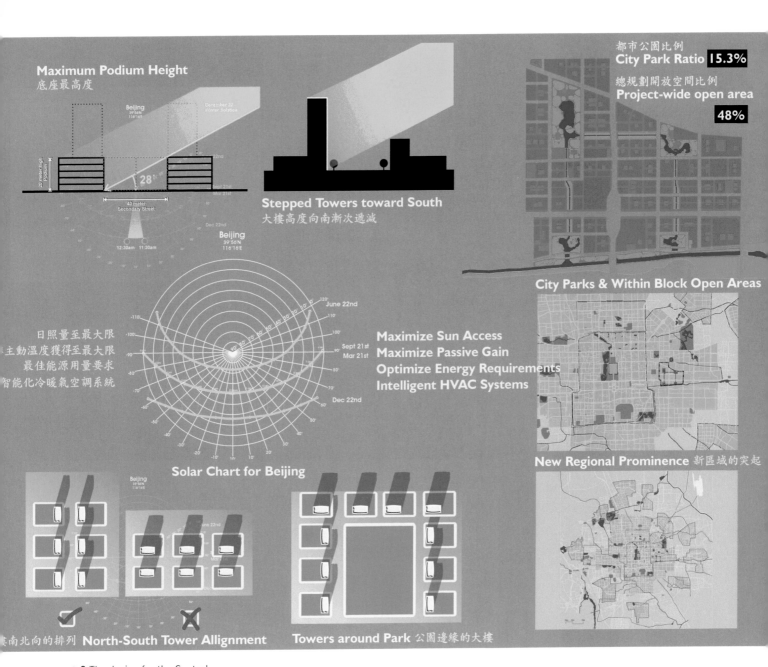

Maximum Podium Height
底座最高度

Beijing
39°56'N
116°16'E

December 22
Winter Solstice

28°

20 meter High Podium

40 meter
Secondary Street

Beijing
39°56'N
116°16'E

12:30am 11:30am

Dec 22nd

Stepped Towers toward South
大樓高度向南漸次遞減

都市公園比例
City Park Ratio `15.3%`

總規劃開放空間比例
Project-wide open area
`48%`

City Parks & Within Block Open Areas

日照量至最大限
主動溫度獲得至最大限
最佳能源用量要求
智能化冷暖氣空調系統

June 22nd

Sept 21st
Mar 21st

Dec 22nd

Beijing
39°56'N
116°16'E

Solar Chart for Beijing

Maximize Sun Access
Maximize Passive Gain
Optimize Energy Requirements
Intelligent HVAC Systems

New Regional Prominence 新區域的突起

Beijing
39°56'N
116°16'E

June 22nd

要南北向的排列 **North-South Tower Allignment**

Towers around Park 公園邊緣的大樓

2.8 The design for the Central
Business District in Beijing
is a major addition to the city.
Open spaces, parks and
roads are oriented in ways that
give buildings direct sunlight
for a minimum of two hours
each day.

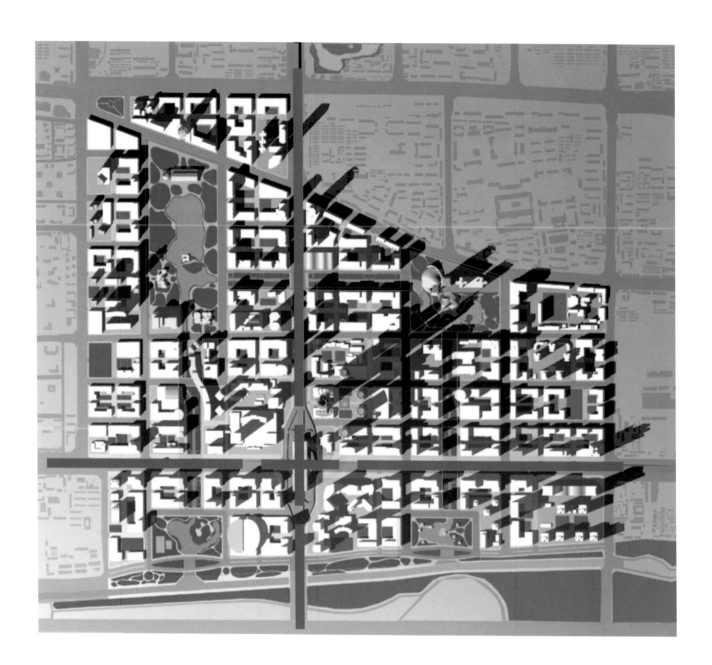

BF Although we have mentioned solar access as a positive example of sustainability in China, the Chinese totally disregard recycling and are very insensitive to historic preservation. During an earlier trip to Beijing, we were walking near the Third Ring Road in southeast Beijing and noticed the outer walls of a well-preserved hutong district. It seemed like a wonderful historic example. A month later, walking the same route, we saw that it had been totally demolished and in its place, still in construction, was a wide arterial road. They are very insensitive about this. So we all have a long way to go.

SJ If they were conscious of their roots, they might pay more attention to that. Sustainability is such an all-encompassing notion that it is, in the end, a reflection of culture. It inevitably defines a culture's sense of balance between what one wants for one's self in one's own time, and what one is willing to share.

69

In the States for example, conversations regarding energy efficiency and sustainability usually devolve to an interrogation over the quantity of stuff that has been specified in order to achieve certain ratings. It's like, Christmas is green this year; what have you got on your list? It's a consumer event. Solar panels, low-flow fixtures, heat exchangers, recycled glass tile. Count up the stuff, and if there's enough, you get a star. While all these devices kick off the discussion of how a building can be operated differently, they are nothing but a primer.

In my view, you can do much more by transforming the views of an informed population into social policy to which architecture and design can then respond. In the case of our Capitol East End project, the political decision to mop up over 40 state offices scattered around ex-urban Sacramento and consolidate them in the challenged inner city is a huge step in support of sustainability. Think of its impact on the strengthening of public transportation systems, the reduction in use of fossil fuels, the choices for childcare, the support for nearby retail, and the rejuvenation and increased security of public open space. These are deeply sustainable moves in addition to what the architecture can achieve.

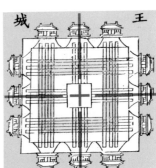

Traditional City Plan, China

CAPITOL AREA EAST END COMPLEX | SACRAMENTO | 1998 | FIGURES 2.10–2.17

2.10 Located at the Eastern terminus of Capitol Park, the Capitol Area East End is an ambitious multi-block mixed-use office-development designed to consolidate the headquarters operations of three departments of California state government. Sixty-four hundred employees of the Departments of Health Services, Education and General Services are housed in the five-building, 1.5 million square foot development, along with 1,500 parking spaces. Public amenities include retail, community police station, 300-seat auditorium, and childcare center with outdoor play area. The Department of Education Building is the largest in the United States to have achieved a Gold LEED™ Rating.

2.11

2.12

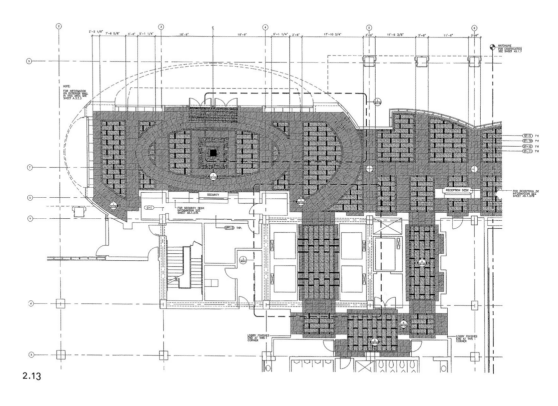

2.13

BF In Sacramento, there was a conscious effort to make the buildings as sustainable as possible, on many levels. We were careful to recycle materials—from salvaged marble, to on-site soil, even the use of fly ash in mixing the cement, so there was a conscious effort and it is recorded in the LEED checklist format.

Questions still arise... What does all of this mean to composing the building and the spaces that surround it? Are there major differences, or is it a matter of detail and process? We are still exploring that. And there is the question of the role of cultural expression. Assuming that it has a role, or can have a role, sustainability begs for an idea that lessons from the past need to be conveyed to the future. It doesn't necessarily draw a line between the abstract vs. the literal, or the universal vs. the regional.

SJ That's why sustainability is such a potentially beautiful departure point for developing form, because it can be neutral in a cultural sense. Sustainability is authentic, achievable, and much needed. Sounds like a legitimate design problem, right?

No green bells and whistles. It's a whole attitude. Childcare. Senior citizens. The health of cities that give us life. How are any of these concerns materially different? We can sit here in downtown Los Angeles while to the east of us there are hundreds of acres of grossly underutilized building stock. What about that? Those buildings could be the basis for a new and different downtown, which frankly could dwarf the present one.

BF The roots of Native America are all about sustainable use of resources. The Indians tend to build in a way that is minimally invasive to the environment. Our Native American Cultural Center and Museum in Oklahoma incorporates sustainability at most levels. It is a part of the belief system of the place. Just the fact that the site was given back to the Indians by the white guys, it was a throwaway, totally depleted of its mineral resources. You will recall that it was a major oil drilling site, and the soils are polluted and the Indians are planning to restore it to its pristine state. There is a kind of irony in this. The story goes that Indians have had to deal with natural processes over the centuries, they have had to survive and adapt, they have had to recycle, and they look to nature for answers. They read nature and adapt to the forces at play in nature. One can only speculate that early China was like this, too.

2.14 Interior spaces are designed with fragmentary references to the Capitol's classical architecture. These fragments become abstractions that are assembled to create a new architectural whole.

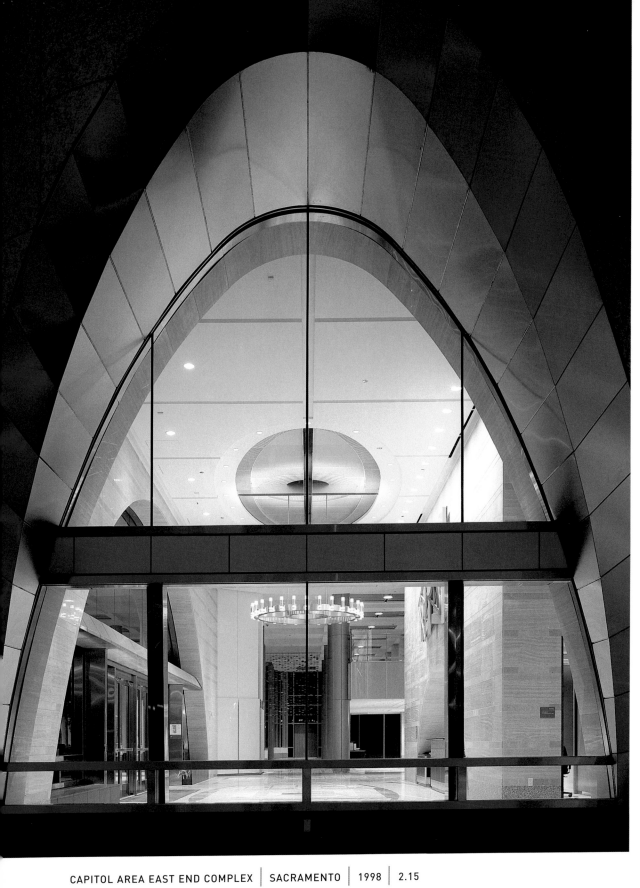

CAPITOL AREA EAST END COMPLEX │ SACRAMENTO │ 1998 │ 2.15

2.16

2.17

2.16 Main lobby entrance with arcade beyond

2.17 Prefunction lobby to auditorium

SJ This is a much more interesting way to talk about sustainability than how many X's in the rating column you got.

BF It's much deeper if sustainability is a part of a society's belief system and consequently the society gives value to it. This becomes an immense help for us designers when making sustainability a fundamental part of our approach—that which is included in the overall concept, which is less dependent upon a technological offset.

SJ As much as we might like to take credit for it, Bill, in reality, these are two projects whose commitment to sustainability actually predates our involvement. With the Native American Cultural Center and Museum, the tribes themselves are historically predisposed to both a reverence for and dependence on the land. Their spirituality grows directly out of that. Then, the Feds toss them a piece of wetlands that has been seriously polluted and largely abandoned and in the grace of their tradition, they accept it, are non-judgmental about it, and begin to carefully plan to re-inhabit it. We could learn from this.

77

BF Another example of sustainability at the planning level is the L.A. Civic Center Facilities Plan. It proposes to get full use out of planned projects and buildings and spaces they already have. With four branches of government in the civic center area of downtown, the idea is to make it more "civic" and less "governmental" by locating shared facilities like cafeterias, cafes, conferencing facilities, day care and other similar uses on public rights-of-way. The idea is to force employees out of buildings into the outdoor spaces that are shared by all. By doing this, it makes this "walled" place more accessible to the average citizen, more a part of the city and consequently more democratic.

SJ As opposed to territorializing each branch and building duplicate facilities.

BF To a degree, we have taken each agency's own facilities and turned them inside out. It leads to a very logical discussion about urban design and how you activate public spaces and how you share those spaces in a specific way.

METROPOLITAN LOFTS | LOS ANGELES | 2003 | FIGURES 2.18–2.20

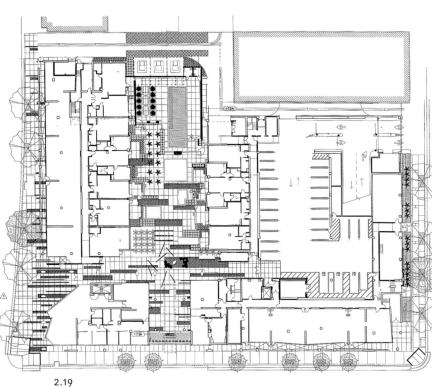

2.19

2.18 Metropolitan Lofts is a
new mixed-use development
with 274 loft apartments, the
first new urban loft building
in downtown Los Angeles. The
8-story concrete and corrugated
steel clad building has large
industrial framed windows,
balconies, open kitchens and
all natural interior finishes.
Residential units are laid out
for proximity to the private
courtyard garden, pool, and
social areas, as well as to maximize views to downtown's
dramatic skyline.

2.19 Ground floor plan
2.20 Site plan

2.20

SJ The ultimate form of recycling, of course, is adaptive reuse in the inner city. We've done a lot of this work in the past, although it frequently falls below the radar of urgent architectural critique because of its mission. But in the end, just how radical or compelling is the term *recycle*? Actually, in this town it's fairly radical, and very new.

The historic Terminal Post Office Annex near Union Station, Pacific Center next to the Biltmore, Robinson's Department Store, Union Bank, the first high-rise building in downtown Los Angeles, and of course, Rincon Center in the heart of San Francisco. We are just now beginning construction on Metropolitan Lofts, a live-work loft apartment building in South Park near the Staples Arena. While this is a new, from-the-ground-up building, it acknowledges two important things. Number one, an underutilized former manufacturing district can achieve new life with the addition of residents, and all the things those residents will need. Number two, like the land for our Native American project, when you redefine the market, new realities and new viabilities are created. It turns out that there is a large cohort of potential residents who don't find the more suburban offerings a satisfactory choice, and they can see possibilities for a residential life downtown where others have not...

Terminal Post Office Annex, Los Angeles

BF ...and the project offers an alternative for those endless parking lots that have surrounded high-rise downtowns across the country.

Another point about sustainability is that it's not a substitute for design. That is, it should be a primary consideration in what we design but it is not a substitute for the creative process and artistic decision made by individual designers. This was evident a few years ago in conversations we had during a collaboration with Bill McDonough, who was regarded as the "green dean" at the University of Virginia, and who has an enormous grasp of the subject and talks about it in very philosophical and practical ways. When you get down to actually designing the building, there is something there that needs to close the gap.

Rincon Center, San Francisco

SJ So we're back to the real world of design. Even the most right-thinking mantra will not procure inspired or even good design. To move beyond program, design must integrate

82

2.21 Located on 250 acres of gentle rolling hills, the Donum Estate is an estate winery and vineyard dedicated to the production of a high quality Pinot Noir.

THE DONUM ESTATE | SONOMA COUNTY | 2001 | FIGURES 2.21–2.24

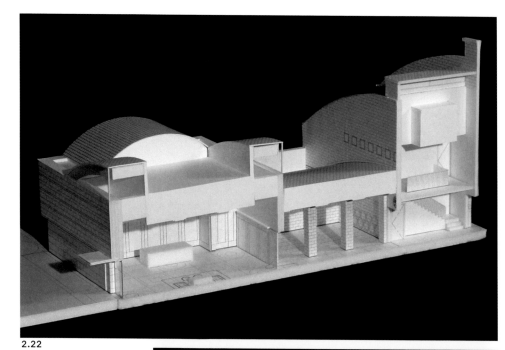

2.22

84

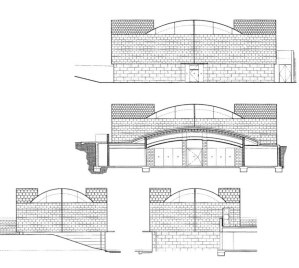

2.23

2.24

2.22 The 28,000 sqft winery combines state of the art small tank fermentation and blending with a historic gravity flow production method.

2.23 Building elevations and sections

2.24 Model

ideas into a total and compelling physical belief system. And, design must engage the intuitive or non-rational psyche of Freud's id, Jacques Derrida's joker, and the radicalization of beauty, in the words of the art critic, Dave Hickey. All describe a place which memorable design must touch. It is this creative conceptual leap we are looking for in the work.

BF And long ago in the art world when Braque and Picasso tried so hard to depersonalize artistic expression, only eventually to succumb to it.

So we get back to the original question, which is whether sustainability can create a different sort of architecture?

Dave Hickey

SJ When the rationality of sustainability is married to the irrationality of beauty, it will have arrived. And it will be different.

BF But will it be fundamentally different? The hope is that it will be, not just having smarter and more thoughtful projects. It does not substitute for a belief system nor does it move the wall of knowledge. Until we decide how to create a new humanistic architecture around it, and about it, sustainability is bound to be about gadgets. It's not, yet, an idea that can stand by itself. It's not just about catching sun rays. And at a societal level, we have to accept that sustainability is fundamentally important. In fact, in the post-industrial world, it might be our salvation, and as it becomes even more economical, people will aggressively convert to its principles. That's the hope.

Jacques Derrida

SJ That conversion is already happening. People are already saying how much you can recover in life-cycle costs.

BF Wait till gasoline goes to four dollars a gallon!

SJ We'll all be bicycling to work. Costs start going up and people start thinking differently. Will SUVs be history?

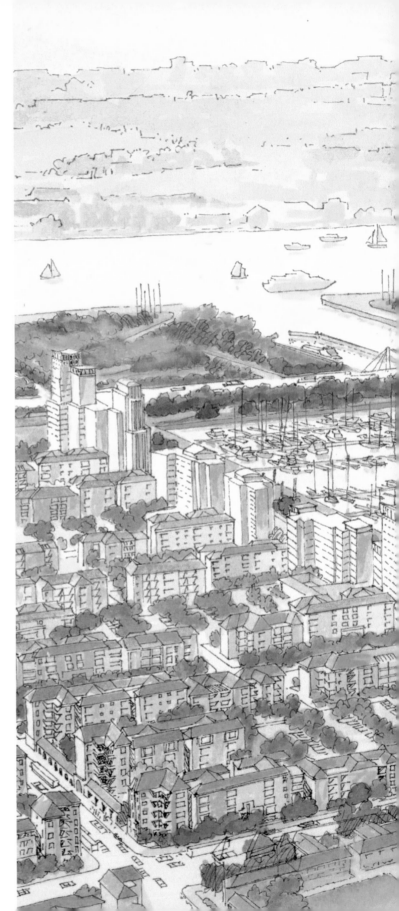

2.25 Located on a former air base in central Shanghai, the ten-square-kilometer area of the Jiangwan New Sub-Town District is designed for a community of 100,000 as a means to relieve growth and redevelopment pressures. The plan is made up of three neighborhoods: a high-density, mixed-use Center to the south; a low-density residential neighborhood planned around a series of open spaces and lakes at the center of the plan; and a Waterfront Development to the north consisting of a mix of mid-and high-rise housing around a network of canals and boat basin connected to the Huangpu River. The plan is based on a social program of improvements in education and sustainability, as well as increasing amounts of leisure time.

SHANGHAI NEW JIANGWAN TOWN | SHANGHAI | 2001 | FIGURES 2.25–2.30

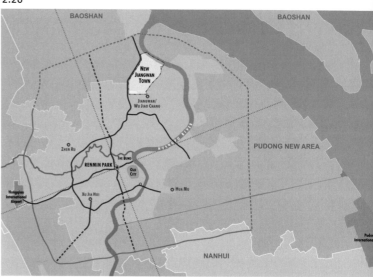

2.26

2.27

2.28

2.28 The three areas are integrated by an ecologically-balanced open space system which offers a variety of opportunities for live, work and recreation. The proposed open space system in conjunction with the road network seamlessly extends the existing fabric of the city into the new town. The plan emphasizes the principles of sustainable design and "transit-first" development setting new standards for the region.

2.26 Location map

2.27 Model, birds eye perspective

SHANGHAI NEW JIANGWAN TOWN │ SHANGHAI │ 2001 │ 2.26–2.28

BF Hope so. If society believes strongly in sustainability and values it, the design of sustainable environments will follow. It's about the natural system where there is harmony between nature and man. In order to survive, man must manage the elements so they work together in natural ways. This brings us back to Native America where earth is valued, whether it is the siting of the museum complex which is dependent on earth mounds to raise the buildings above the floodwaters of the river, the restoration of the soil's pristine state, or acknowledgment of natural elements—earth, wind, water and fire. To Native America the symbolism represents an inseparable belief between values and actions.

SJ The four elements. The same elements as in Plato's *Timaeus*. Don't believe the two parties ever met, though.

89

BF How do *you* know?

SJ Which brings us back to seeing things as transcendent that, in our current Western mindset, we are not guided to see as transcendent. We talked earlier about the relativity of words, concepts and activities in Native American life. Two examples have always impressed me from our meetings with tribal elders. One is the fact that from time to time, an elder would refer to a relative by name as if he were in the room in the present tense, and you'd find yourself looking around wondering which one he was. Only later would you realize that this relative was long deceased, and the elder conceived him to still be living in some form and omnipresent in the here and now.

Another memorable event was the prayer of another tribal elder who was asked to give thanks for the food prior to a lunch meeting. He raised both hands skyward, closed his eyes, and thanked the father of us all for providing, thanked the spirits of nature which had delivered the food to us, and asked that with it, and our deeds, we all contribute to the eternal circle of life. With that, he closed the prayer "in the name of Jesus Christ. Amen." We began by listening to a native prayer, and finished by hearing a Christian blessing.

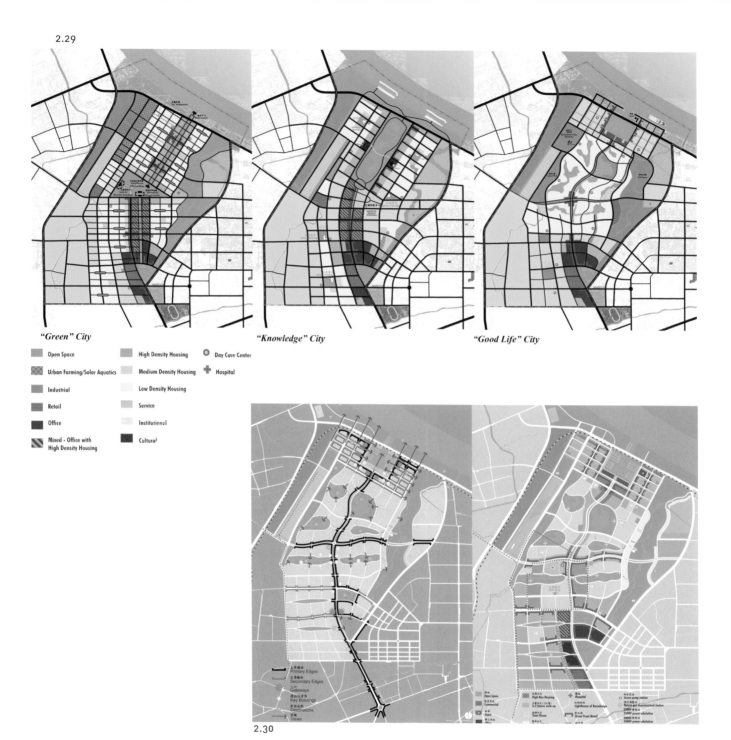

"Green" City

"Knowledge" City

"Good Life" City

Open Space
Urban Farming/Solar Aquatics
Industrial
Retail
Office
Mixed - Office with High Density Housing

High Density Housing
Medium Density Housing
Low Density Housing
Service
Institutional
Cultural

Day Care Center
Hospital

2.30

2.29 Three concept alternatives

2.30 The plan is made up of three neighborhoods; a high-density, mixed-use sub town center to the south; a low-density residential neighborhood planned around a series of open spaces and lakes at the center and the waterfront development to the north consisting of a mix of mid and high-rise housing around a network of canals.

BF Native Americans have several themes that they abide by. One of them is the theme of adaptation. A good many Native Americans are Christian and they see nothing wrong with that. There is something about the culture they live in and its spiritual heritage that brings about an intersection between Christ and their spirituality. That spirituality is different but Indians have adapted Christianity to it. The sensitivities to certain qualities in nature are different. That's why in the plan for the Native American Center in Oklahoma there has been an effort to integrate the earth and the building. It's an engagement of the two in an almost seamless way. They believe that life carries on after death, and that mankind really came from the earth and transcends to heaven after death, so the idea of Jesus Christ and the Christian afterlife is not incompatible with that belief.

SJ So for us, this alternate universe, this different orientation to the sacred, was a tonic, and a great gift.

    The great religions all look for a constant and immutability in the human spirit, an eternal transcendent something, which each religion defines in its own way. What is common to them all is the search for this transcendence, and that is the ultimate sense of sustainability. In the end, it is a spiritual idea. I want to bring back the word "sustainability" in a conceptual way—not in a grocery list way—and practice sustainability as an inter-generational idea, as an idea about cities and their longevity and their re-use...

BF ...according to the Native Americans, for at least seven generations.

91

2.31 The house is designed for a family of five and is located on a site overlooking the Pacific Ocean in Malibu, California. The configuration of rooms is linear and parallels the coastline in an attempt to provide a wide range of views. The central feature of the house is the double story rotunda living room with a 22 foot glass wall overlooking the ocean. Arrival to the house is from a motor court at the upper level along with bedrooms and private spaces. The kitchen, dining and other social spaces are below, extending out to the generous pool deck to the rear.

PRIVATE RESIDENCE | MALIBU, CALIF. | 1997 | FIGURES 2.31–2.35

PRIVATE RESIDENCE │ MALIBU, CALIF. │ 1997 │ 2.32

PRIVATE RESIDENCE │ MALIBU, CALIF. │ 1997 │ 2.33

PRIVATE RESIDENCE | MALIBU, CALIF. | 1997 | 2.35

DNA OF THE CITY
IMPROVISATION and the URBAN GRID

BF Before coming to Southern California in the early 80s, both Scott and I worked on a number of projects that involved a high degree of public benefit. In Scott's case, his work with Philip Johnson on the Republic Bank Building in Houston and the Times Square project in New York City, while in my case, in New York City's Urban Design Group under Jacquelin Robertson, which Jon Barnett wrote about in *Urban Design as Public Policy*. The important point about this is that we are accustomed to public issues and understand the public process. I think this makes our office a little different from others.

Republic Bank Center, Houston

SJ That's an important connection. Although we are getting more public commissions now, even our private work is frequently large-scale work with a big impact on the public realm, so we regard these kinds of projects philosophically as *de facto* public work.

BF Exactly right. Urban design projects, whether they are for private or public clients, must resolve conflicting issues involving traffic, open space, pedestrian linkages, land assemblage, the height of new structures, to mention a few. This is inevitably a big part of planning in a capitalist economy, which depends heavily upon a regulated free market. So, we would like to think that as a result of our urban design solutions, everyone is better off, but this is near impossible. Christine Boyer coined an expression a number of years ago which more accurately describes this effort to resolve conflict, as *Pareto optimality*; which means that some interests may gain as a result of a plan, but no one loses. So there is probably a whole body of people in certain situations that really don't benefit or lose. They are left in a neutral position. Kissinger used the term a lot with regard to politics.

Christine Boyer

Given our political structure and the public debate that often occurs around major projects, design is an effort to resolve conflict, such as can often be seen between

100

3.1 The Los Angeles house sits on a tight urban lot and draws upon the implicit grid of the city to define the building.

PRIVATE RESIDENCE | LOS ANGELES | 1999 | FIGURES 3.1–3.6

1. BEDROOM
2. GALLERY
3. STUDY
4. ROOF DECK

THIRD FLOOR PLAN

1. LIVING
2. DINING
3. KITCHEN
4. MASTER BEDROOM
5. WARDROBE
6. POOL

SECOND FLOOR PLAN

1. ENTRY VESTIBLE
2. LIBRARY
3. GUEST ROOM
4. STORAGE
5. PARKING
6. POOL

GROUND FLOOR PLAN

3.2

102

3.3 "The semantic variations... take the spatial envelope of the house as a point of departure for a series of surprises that follow."

3.3

the perceived public good of a community group versus the private gain of a developer. There is an inherent conflict between those two issues, and it goes to basic constitutional issues regarding our rights as individuals versus the things we share in common. Urban design or planning frameworks attempt to resolve these conflicts in the urban context. We seek to create plans that benefit everyone, but we can't guarantee it. There are certain things that are difficult to resolve in ways in which everyone benefits. But at very least we try to achieve an optimal condition. So, in this sense, you are trying to resolve conflicts in society, and you are trying to propose measures that resolve issues of traffic and density and light and air and open space. What you try to seek is this level of optimality that resolves the conflicts in a way in which some people benefit but no one is the clear loser.

SJ It's like the Hippocratic Oath of urban design, "First, do no harm."

BF It's a difficult goal, but it's what we seek to achieve. When we do urban design and planning, we try to recognize and establish the appropriate level of intervention or levels of control. In other words, we can try to create structures inside which others can make decisions and we try to control or influence those decisions. It's not intended to be unilateral or dictatorial, even though it may end up that way in some cases, but usually it is quite open-ended. These structures are democratic, but at the same time there are mandates that ensure the integrity of the overall urban design plan and assure levels of public benefit.

Another point about our urban design work is that we are not wedded to any particular dogmas, and there are many of those around, such as the New Urbanism. New Urbanism promotes certain qualities regarding human scale and spatial clarity that we support wholeheartedly, but we see the practice of urban design as one that should not necessarily presuppose a kind of dogma. For us it needs to be much more open-ended. We feel that our plans need to be of our time. We use our research to recall memory, not nostalgia. The structures we derive allow contemporary expression, whether at Mission Bay, Jiangwan Sub-town Center, the Native American Center or the San Francisco Piers. All have come from a process that recalls memory, creates a collage of narratives, respects history while eroding it, and offers the client a strategy in our search for content. Solutions come out of analysis and an understanding of the particular urban condition.

PRIVATE RESIDENCE | LOS ANGELES | 1999 | 3.4

PRIVATE RESIDENCE │ LOS ANGELES │ 1999 │ 3.6

We feel that we are designing cities, or parts of cities, where the materials and methods include market assumptions, land-use zoning, transportation systems and public workshops, open space, housing and employment and certain environmental factors, in addition to standards for building materials and finishes. In other words, an urban designer must have knowledge that is different from that of the traditional building designer. Although urban design follows essentially the same process as architecture, urban designers use different kinds of information.

SJ Bill has opened up the issue of how architecture and urban design are similar and how they are different and the dialectic that exists between the two. Certainly we share the view that design should have a public purpose, even if it has a private sponsor. As an office, we view the design product as a response to the public interest. In urban design and planning, the goal may be to circle the wagons of a large group of stakeholders and reach a consensus. In architecture, you may well enter the process with a consensus as a starting point, which you can accept or revise or reject either out of the need to challenge assumptions or the need to design to an evolving program. Design guidelines or standards that are generalized in a master plan may not foster the most democratic or expressive architecture.

This is also a question of figure/ground. There is, on the one hand, a need to establish an identifiable DNA, as Bill calls it, to way-finding within the city, and, on the other hand, there is the need to create meaningful aberrations within the master plan that privilege other worthy social or natural features.

BF I am of the belief that one of the greatest failures of architects and urban designers in the 20th Century has been addressing the issue of scale in our cities. Right now, programs are given to the designer after developers and lenders make decisions regarding size. These decisions tend to reflect the current trends of global capital to aggregate land in larger and larger formations, which in turn necessitates the construction of very large buildings on large sites. This is a phenomenon that happens in both public projects, like government centers, and in private development. It is all too easy for the designer to follow the lead of these well-capitalized clients and design projects that are more and more self-contained, like shopping centers or other mega-structures, that have little

107

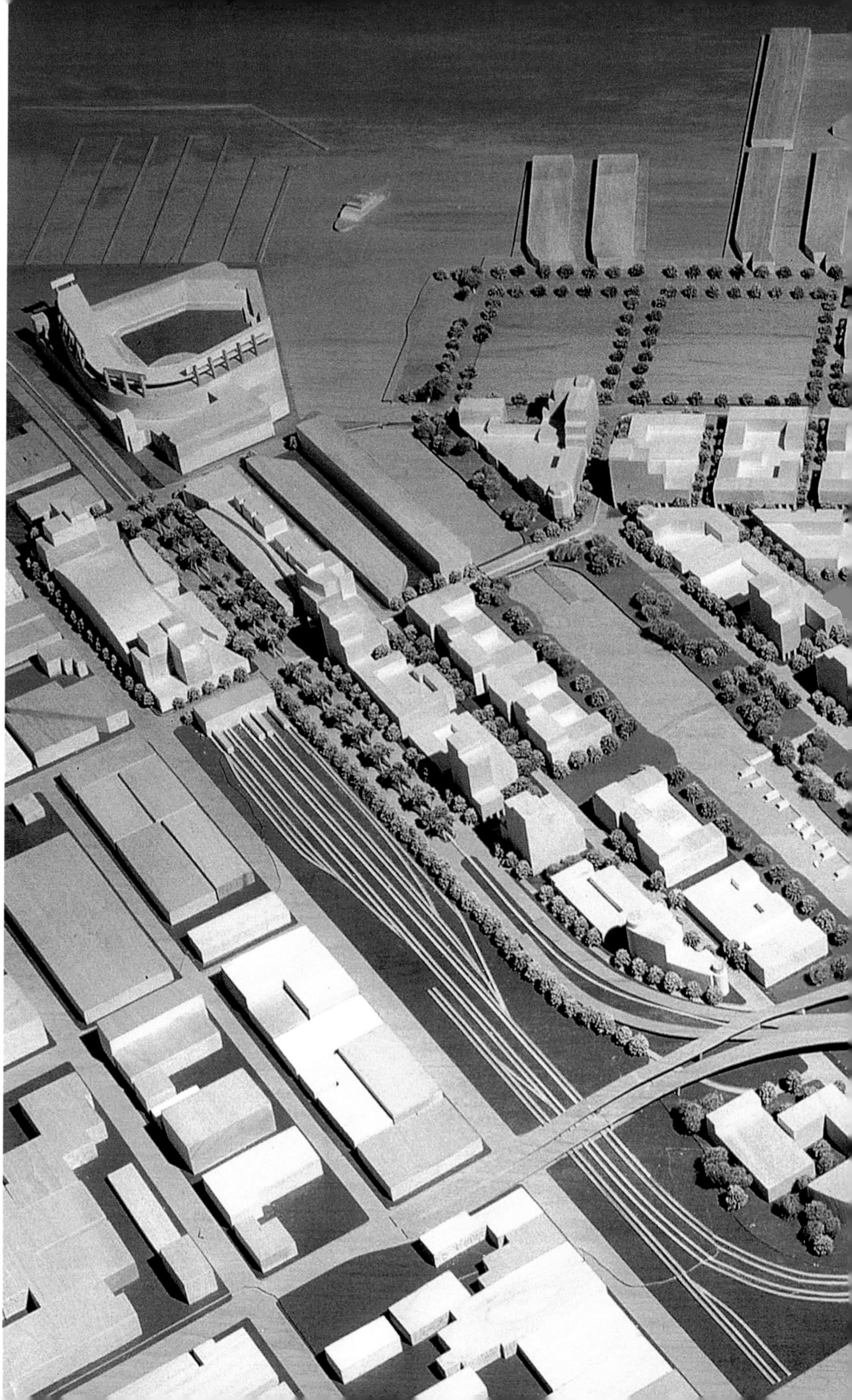

MISSION BAY MASTER PLAN | SAN FRANCISCO | 1999 | FIGURES 3.7–3.10

3.8

3.9

3.7 Mission Bay is an urban mixed-use neighborhood that integrates and extends San Francisco's open space system, and street framework, the latter based on the historic "Vara" block dating from 1839. Basic plan principles include: Orientation to water; Integration of North and South of Channel developments via a series of open spaces; Location of lower scaled elements at the water; Mandate for buildings to act as street walls; and the creation of an urban neighborhood.

The University of California at San Francisco is located at the heart of the plan playing a central role in the plan structure and distribution of land uses. The plan strives to integrate commercial, research and development, and university uses with a balanced mixture of market and affordable housing.

3.8 Violet used Vara Blocks to lay out the first six blocks of San Francisco in 1839. Johnson Fain identified it as the "DNA" of the city.

MISSION BAY MASTER PLAN | **SAN FRANCISCO** | **1999** | **3.8, 3.9**

regard for the city as a whole. Many times the design of these places seems to monu-mentalize the ego of the architect as much as the project itself. Places like Moscone Center, for instance, aggregate a number of sites into a block that is so large that a person loses the sense of scale of the surrounding city. You lose the smallness of San Francisco for no apparent benefit. In Berlin, the Sony Center in Potsdammer Platz suffers from the same problem, whereas across the street, Renzo Piano's project addresses the city quite appropriately. In New York City the Fifth Avenue Special Zoning District done in the 70s tried to re-introduce small scale or human scale to the grid by punching pathways through mid-block locations, so pedestrians would not be forced to walk all the way around a block that is 800 feet long if they took a wrong turn.

All this is to say that urban design is complex and can take different forms of expression, depending upon the problem at hand. In giving structure to a large, multi-block project, the plan must allow for flexibility in our diverse society. Decisions can become more democratic and less dictatorial. The issue comes down to a very simple notion; you have to develop on a piece of property of a certain size, and these decisions will affect others around you, so you need an approach that allows flexibility within the context of the overall system. If you are dependent upon on a single decision to make your project work, or to make your city work, you are in trouble. The city is really the aggregation of many decisions. The system must allow for quite a diverse set of development decisions to occur over a long period of time. The structure needs to have integrity and open-

Potsdammer Platz, Berlin

endedness. In that sense, the structure must be universal and may in fact be the deep structure of the city. So there is something problematic, something anti-urban when developers want to depart from the universal system, and make larger and larger land assemblages that are more and more self-enclosed. Irvine is an example of that.

SJ That's right. The case of Irvine may be an example of how the nature of architectural decision-making can be a poor approach to urban design. We've spoken about the

3.10 "On the scale of the city,
a grid takes a lot of participation.
When you lay out the grid,
you are laying out a structure
that owners and developers
and architects will respond to,
in some cases, for generations.
It will allow the full range
of choices to be exercised in
the city."

PRIVATE RESIDENCE | RUTHERFORD, CALIF. | 1998 | FIGURES 3.11–3.8

3.11 "The Rutherford house... is less about enclosure and more about horizontal continuity between spaces and views throughout the house..."

3.12

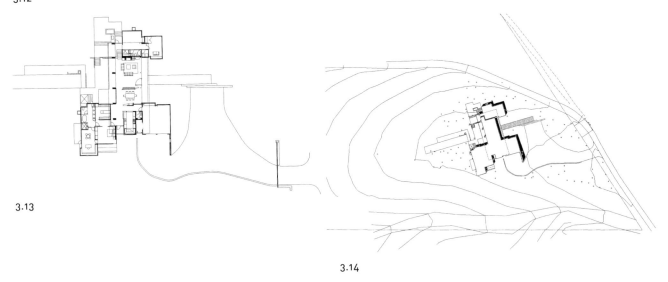

3.13

3.14

3.12 The outside and inside of the house are seemingly locked together.

opposite problem, but Bill is right: Urban design is more than just big architecture.
A certain kind of idealism or self-reference might produce a compelling work of architecture, no matter how fictitious it really is. However, these same qualities of isolation and inflexibility may be deadly for urban design.

BF I'll give you an example. A number of years ago, we did a plan at Mission Bay for Nelson Rising at Catellus. Ours was the fifth version of the site plan in 20 years. We ended up doing some research into the history of San Francisco, trying to get a better understanding of the city, and out of that we proposed the simple idea of using Vara blocks in a grid and orienting the grid to support view corridors towards the Bay and toward downtown. We re-introduced the Vara block, which the colonial surveyors had used, as the DNA of the city. The Vara block was traditional; Vioget used it to lay out the first six blocks of downtown San Francisco in 1839.

117

We laid out Mission Bay using these traditionally dimensioned city blocks, and developed guidelines to establish the scale of the neighborhood. Then we helped the developer negotiate with UC San Francisco to bring the university's new biotechnology campus into the center of the project. Mission Bay is 300 acres and the campus is 47 acres inside of that. UC decided to hold a competition for their campus design—a kind of plan within a plan—and selected five architects for the competition. We "scoped" the project for the competing firms, and gave them the structure within which to make their plans. Later we sat in the jury for the competition.

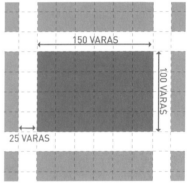

The Vara Block

Steven Holl, one of the participants, from day one decided he was going to challenge the whole idea of the grid and throw it out. After two months, he finally came to the jury, and said that he had struggled with a number of ideas, and in the end he came back to the grid. He admitted in the presentation that he had discovered the grid had given him freedom, which he had never imagined. The scheme was spatially very interesting. He drew distinction between a Modernist idea of spatial organizational and a traditional urban scheme, and he played them against each other. Another participant proposed a New Urbanist scheme that dealt with the grid well, although it was quite

PRIVATE RESIDENCE │ RUTHERFORD, CALIF. │ 1998 │ 3.15

3.16 Individual rooms are
loosely defined, the house
is opened up.

PRIVATE RESIDENCE | RUTHERFORD, CALIF. | 1998 | 3.16

3.17

3.18

3.17, 3.18 Rear and side elevations.

literal, but the proposed architecture was overly historicist. So it shows that using the 19th Century grid is very equitable, very flexible and open-ended. You had two schemes on this grid, one by the New Urbanists who interpreted the Vara block in a very literal way and translated the architecture into brick and Victorian references, versus another team that was more artistic and who initially tried to challenge the grid, but who ultimately came back to the street system and constructed a Modernist spatial idea inside of it. It goes to show, you can do Modernist architecture on a traditional grid. It also illustrates that others can design imaginatively within the structure of the urban design plan.

SJ I often think that some of the most brilliant urban designs are the simplest, which is an odd thing, if you think about it. The design for a simple object like a coffee cup can be simple because it doesn't have much work to do. And yet Mission Bay is a huge idea, a 300-acre idea, and yet the concept is perfectly appropriate for urban design. It's funny how simplicity can often work at both very small and very large scales.

BF Well, a simple expression can be very complex, but a simple idea need not be simplistic. Mission Bay is an interesting case. The plan is deferential to the city as a whole. It's not trying to separate itself from the city and say, 'this is me.' Instead, it is taking a position that it is very much a part of the city, and relies on its connection to the city.

SJ The history of Modernism, as we all know, has not been very deferential. Nor has it been predominantly about connection. Its roots were in the realm of architecture as revolution. The historic modern building was an object in undifferentiated, infinite space with the implied self-importance of all that. Figure/ground lost its traditional meaning and became ambiguous. What's interesting from an architectural standpoint, is that a truly modern building in the grid can choose to be figure OR ground.

BF As for figure/ground, the grid is spatially neutral. All that the grid provides is an inter-connecting order for buildings and open spaces. The grid acknowledges something important. This takes us back to the problem of bigness. Where some developers try to aggregate large land assemblages and make them into enormous blocks, we took the opposite approach at Mission Bay. We took a very large parcel and disaggregated it.

121

PRIVATE RESIDENCE | LOS ALTOS HILLS, CALIF. | 2000 | FIGURES 3.19–3.25

3.19 This 6,800 square foot single story home is located high above the southern end of the San Francisco Bay in the Los Altos Hills. Located on a 12-acre site, the house represents a substantial expansion and remodel of an important modern house designed in the mid-1950's by John Funk and featured in Sally Woodbridge's Bay Area Houses. The new design preserves all primary steel structure and window frames, the principal ceiling plane, and the original thermal concrete floor slab which ran throughout the original house. Major materials in the house are stacked desert flagstone for all hearths and fireplaces, custom wood millwork in quartersawn North American maple and macassar ebony, and hand-finished and colored radiant concrete floor. Wall finishes are steel troweled sandless plaster; new skylight monitors are lined in maple with north-facing clear plate glass. Glass mosaic tile, natural cork wall covering and stainless steel hardware and fittings describe an environment which is both natural and durable.

3.20 View from interior.

We did it in a way that was equitable, that is, the blocks were equal size and dimensions, even though it is an irregular site. What happens is that interposing the grid on the land becomes a method of ensuring a certain scale of development within the grid. We had a big debate with UC San Francisco, because they wanted to build some very large buildings on some very large blocks, but in the end we convinced them to respect the grid. At the campus design for UC San Francisco, in several cases you see multiple buildings planned within a single block. So the grid does help break down bigness in the city. What the smaller block does is disaggregate buildings. That's why it is important to retain the street system. It preserves city scale.

The Vara turns out to be an ideal size for urban design and development. In Portland, in comparison, the blocks are 200 feet by 200 feet. That's too small for development; subterranean parking can't work on a block that small, because there is not enough space for vehicular ramps. The Vara block, at 275 feet by 412 feet, is large enough for parking and still compact enough to be walkable for pedestrians.

125

SJ Many of our smaller projects are also organized on the principal of a grid. Take our residential work, for example. They show how the grid is an open semantic form, if you will, and it can be used syntactically to articulate very different spatial concepts. The St. Helena house, for example, brings the grid into the third axis, which is to say, the vertical. This move is used to create a series of cubic volumes separated by slices of transparency, which gives a distinct articulation to each volume. This same move allows direct interior views of the landscape between rooms. The Rutherford house uses the grid typically in only two axes and is less about enclosure than it is about creating horizontal continuity between spaces and views throughout the house, as a means to lock the outside and inside together. This approach has the effect of opening up the house rather than defining individual rooms.

Finally, the Los Angeles house sits on a tight urban lot and draws upon the implicit grid of the city to define the building. Here, the footprint of the house per se corresponds almost exactly to the long-standing pattern of residential lots, which in turn gives it a strong relationship to the street grid and neighboring lots. The semantic variations, or figures, take the spatial envelope of the house as a point of departure for a series of surprises that follow.

PRIVATE RESIDENCE | LOS ALTOS HILLS, CALIF. | 2000 | 3.21

3.22

3.23

3.21 View of longitudinal gallery
3.22 Family kitchen
3.23 Living room

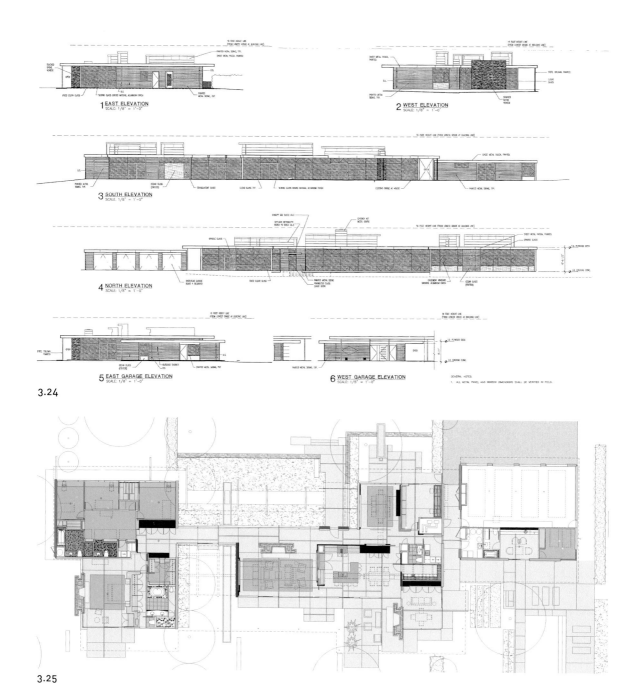

3.24

3.25

3.25 New floor plan

BF On the scale of the city, a grid takes a lot of participation. When you lay out the grid, you are laying out a structure that owners and developers and architects will have to respond to, in some cases, for generations. If the grid is designed correctly, however, it will allow the full range of choices to be exercised in the city.

SJ If I may, I'd like to introduce an analogy from another form of language—music. Music is a formal language. Now, how do you achieve beauty in music? Let's look at a quintessentially American version of music, which is jazz.

Now this discussion could apply equally well, I think, to the early Blue Note recordings of the 40s as it can to the present day. There seems to be general agreement in jazz that for a given piece there are a defined number of players, all of whom happen to be listeners as well as performers. Certain elements of their language they hold in common, while others are left open to improvisation. These forms can vary widely, as we know, but the musicians are likely as not to agree on a tonality, what we call a key signature, or a scale, that is, a range of notes that form the tonal structure for the piece. They also agree on a tempo, or a rhythm, which they will lay down for the piece. And they may agree on an overall length, or number of bars that constitute the whole piece, or increments of the piece that recur, and those places where each musician may enter and improvise. Now, there is nothing God-given about this creative contract among jazz musicians, and we know that contracts can be written in infinitely different ways. Still, there is a place in jazz for commonality or agreement or community, if you will, and there is a place for individual expression. All of which sounds like a lesson for designers.

BF But the improv is the really interesting thing.

SJ Well, both the structure and the improv are interesting. The improv can only exist because the structure exists. They are codependent. And we know the line between the two can be drawn differently. Dissonant or unnatural tones that do not belong to the conventional scale can be used for expressive effect, something Thelonious Monk explored. Counter rhythms can be superimposed over primary rhythms, as minimalist composers like Reich and Glass showed us, and now, Rap and Hip-Hop artists are

129

130

3.26 A parking structure for
a waterfront aquarium
is enlivened with whimsical
aquatic imagery such as
rising bubbles on the screen
covering the decks, and
the suggestion of unfurled sails
on the stairwell.

QUEENSWAY BAY PARKING STRUCTURE | LONG BEACH, CALIF. | 1996 | FIGURES 3.26–3.30

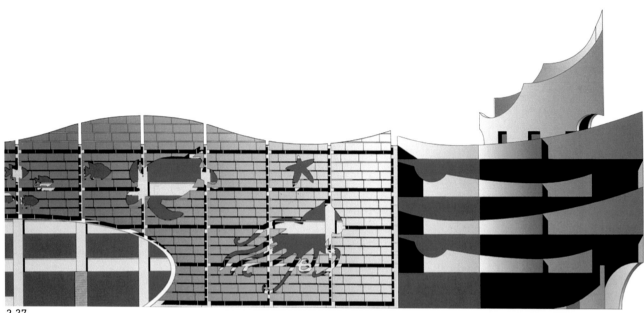

3.27

3.27 "Sea life in profile and a tectonic wave—a conception of beauty and a dialectic between structure and improvisation."

3.28

showing us again. And experimental musicians from John Cage forward have challenged the conventional notion of musical time as a continuous narrative form, and offered us an alternative notion of musical space as a sample from an unpredictable and continuous environment of everyday sound.

BF Even in jazz, there are challenges to structure. Take the saxophonist Sam Rivers, for example. When in Rome, I took jazz CDs with me. That's all I listened to in the studio, and it was fabulous. I started out listening to all the classic recordings and in the end, all I listened to—or listened at—was Sam Rivers. A lot of Sam Rivers. It was so 'improv,' so 'outside,' that it verged on being structureless. But the sound is of our own time.

John Cage

SJ You're describing a sound that mirrors the age, in its search for new forms or no form at all. It sounds challenging.

BF Sam Rivers is challenging, believe me.

SJ I consider Ornette Coleman challenging.

BF Rivers is not a player like Stanley Turrentine or Ernie Watts. He's not something to sit down and relax with. But his music is beautiful in its own way.

SJ We were talking about a conception of beauty which is a product in some way of a dialectic between structure and improvisation.

Sam Rivers

BF Well, what do we mean by beauty? Because, in the case of Sam Rivers, the music is very complex and sounds almost fragmented. For most people, it's just noise.

SJ So he challenges the more comfortable notions people have about narrative sound.

BF At the same time, it is comprehensible.

3.29

3.30

3.30 "The designer may borrow
notions from other media,
but in the end, the work of the
designer is physical."

SJ So people are able to absorb it and make sense out of it?

BF We have absorbed it and feel in harmony with it.

SJ So, does Sam Rivers represent your ideal of urban design, Bill—insofar as his music has been absorbed and represents a consensus?

BF Yes, if a particular site plan is really 'with it.'

SJ This notion of design and music and language each being the product of a dialectic between structure and improvisation, is an interesting one. In architecture or urban design, the response of the designer to the deep structure of a place can, I think, be conceptual, or may borrow notions from other media, but in the end the work of the designer is physical. The piers project in San Francisco has a very apparent deep structure of "finger piers" that extend perpendicularly from the waterfront. Piers, after all, are generally quite similar in form.

Our YMCA pier building, however, is a slightly tortured, even idiosyncratic structure. The traditional "head house," which is the front portion of the pier building as seen from the street, is modern but still well-behaved and typologically clear, while the continuation of the building that spreads out over the pier has much strange work to do. The building is like an overstuffed Halloween bag that spills out here and there to exhibit the exuberant variety of its contents. From a design perspective, we have tried to create a middle place here that bridges the gap between convention and expression, tradition and originality, mask and psyche.

135

CONTROL and CONSENSUS
is it ARCHITECTURE, URBAN DESIGN, or JUST ART?

BILL FAIN I would like to talk about an approach to design which our office is uniquely structured to do. This would be possible because of the relationship between our two disciplines and their distinct foci. It is particularly difficult to *promote* a central idea in urban design. You encounter certain inherent problems when designing at the scale of the city. The urban landscape is also a business landscape and a regulatory landscape. Conditions are not totally under your control, nor are the constraints of the marketplace or politics such that they allow the designer the freedom to determine the best possible solutions. Perhaps this is why current urban design research is directed towards establishing the "big idea" or "concept" for a project. With a big idea, we have some control over coming up with identity, innovation, or a creative expression. Or perhaps that is why we keep coming back to open-ended structures like the grid, which allow for many possible urban scenarios.

SCOTT JOHNSON What Bill has just said is perhaps our ticket to a conversation about the relationship between urban design and architecture. Are they different disciplines, related, or the same? On a practical level, we have already described how I operate at one pole in the office and Bill operates at the other. But there is also no question that there is an overlap, or a "middle ground." I believe this poses a constant tension, or even struggle, and at the same time is a source of considerable strength in those projects that involve both sides of the office. Let me explain.

     While Bill and I share many values (a concern for the vitality of cities, their relation to global trends, and ultimately, the creation of physical environments), Bill is generally trying to create form out of a process that involves consensus building from an enormous number of participants or stakeholders. Like the conductor of the symphony, you can do a better job of it if you play the instruments yourself, or at least know what to expect from each instrument, and each score, and then you must guide the orchestra knowledgeably, and give shape to the music. Bill does this exceptionally well. He has talked about appropriate deference to the existing city, to history, to the flexibility that allows many participants to intervene over time. He has talked about "centering"

SAN FRANCISCO PIERS 27–31 | SAN FRANCISCO | 2002 | FIGURES 4.1–4.7

139

4.1 The redevelopment of Piers 27, 29–31 on San Francisco's Embarcadero waterfront is a public-private joint venture between the Mills Corporation and the YMCA to create recreational opportunities on the waterfront. The project serves all ages and cultural groups, provides opportunities for active and passive recreational activities, and extends the city-wide network of usable public open space along the Embarcadero. The transformation of the Northeast Waterfront from light industry to mixed-use office and commercial uses opens the door of the Bay to the public. The new YMCA building is a update of the historic bulkhead-and-finger-pier building type, providing a wide range of public recreational amenities.

4.2 The YMCA pier building is "a tortured...even idiosyncratic structure...The building is like an overstuffed Halloween bag that spills out here and there to exhibit the exubrant variety of its contents..."

4.3 Site plan of the new pier. The configuration of the new building recalls the historic orientation of the previous piers.

as a concept for both creating a physical place and as a metaphor for public agreement and consent. He has talked about the research that enables him to enter this kind of conversation and to guide it.

But I believe that, *in extremis*, many, or all, of these terms that Bill uses in the context of urban design have a different meaning in the context of architecture such as research, deference, metaphor, and so on. We are back to foundational semantics and the relativity of language.

When there is a call for urban designers, for example, to compete for a new large-scale project at Ground Zero in Lower Manhattan, nine teams are chosen, of which only one considers itself an urban design firm *per se*. The eight others are well-known architects. When an urban design plan is published by, let's say, Michael Sorkin, Thom Mayne, or Rem Koolhaas, the plan has an identifiable formalism consistant with each's architectural work. While I greatly admire much of their architecture, it is hard not to think that what we are seeing is one more "blue painting" from the "blue period,"— that is, one more product from a highly personalized vision—in lieu of any urban design or planning as we think of it here in our studio. When Herbert Muschamp takes up his pen to castigate New York City for tolerating years of banal urban architecture, which he has often done, and with which I agree, he voices a longing for a galvanizing, even willful project. He seems to believe that such a project would serve the city not through functionality or grace but by providing a much needed metaphor that would open a view into a mysterious and alternative universe, one which would be a view into our common, non-rational subconscious. He seems to be looking for a kind of urban poetry that is perhaps more art than urban design, a kind of admission on his part that the two are not the same thing.

It has always struck me that the typical relationship of architecture to urban design hinges on a central confusion regarding territory. I believe there is a war going on from each side for the middle ground. And it is much misunderstood.

To begin with, research in architecture and urban design can be quite different, and serve different needs. Research in architecture, as opposed to the kind of research one does in urban design, might be in the universe of images of, for example, things that are long and low and viewed at 70 miles per hour. Or perhaps we're conducting research into spaces that are taller than they are wide. Or maybe different ways of stringing rooms

141

4.4

4.5

4.4 North elevation
4.5 South side elevation

4.4 North elevation
4.5 South side elevation

SAN FRANCISCO PIERS 27–31 | SAN FRANCISCO | 2002 | 4.4, 4.5

144

4.7

4.6 Rendering of bird's eye perspective of YMCA building.

4.7 The historic piers (upper right) showing "bulkheads" or front elevations of piers, which represent the formal interface between the piers and the cityscape.

together in a processional. The concept of deference, in an architectural sense, might refer to isolating a building as an object, and setting it lightly on the ground in order to leave the surroundings untouched. As for the concept of metaphor, critiques of architecture are now so frequently informed by the vocabulary of post-structuralism and semiotics as to suggest that architecture is inherently metaphoric. Planning and urban design, on the other hand, tend to be critiqued in terms of their ability to provide services, accessibility, and social and economic equity. While good architecture is generally thought to solve problems in creative ways, great architecture is said to convey likeness to other areas of human endeavor and thought. In fact, great architecture seems not to exist without this fixation on the idea beyond, and in addition to, the physical fact of itself. So there are different forces operating here between architecture and urban design.

BF All that's true, but the differences may not be as great as you have portrayed them. Even if architecture is not cloaked as a response to a call to "service," and certainly it can be, and is, critiqued for its social and economic impacts. I would like to think that great urban design and great architecture are inseparable, and, in fact, one feeds the other in ways that hint at forms of universality. Perhaps this is made more difficult because individual works of architecture often seem at times to be more highly resolved and orderly than any given urban scheme. Further, most people may find it difficult to think of individual buildings and the city as operating in a continuum, as a vast hive of spaces. For what it is worth, I have always regarded urban design as the art of designing cities in which the goal is to provide observers with enough information about the city as to enable them to make a creative leap into a larger understanding and appreciation. So, in fact, there is a connection between architecture and urban design, after all. Both require imagination from their designers and active appreciation from observers.

As for the World Trade Center, Fred Schwartz was right. Transferring much of the density away from the site would have made at least as big a difference to the competing schemes as reestablishing the original road through the site did. Otherwise, the task for those involved was reduced to merely clothing the enormous boxes of office space. The two finalists were selected, I believe, because they addressed the aspect of memory on the site—the memorial aspect.

145

AMGEN, INC. BUILDING 38 | THOUSAND OAKS, CALIF. | 1999 | FIGURES 4.8–4.12

4.8 Amgen's Building 38, along with Buildings 27 and 28 (also designed by Johnson Fain) form the administrative complex at Amgen Center. Ground floor employee amenities include a Conference Center, retail, café and two-level fitness center. The building features stone and glass exteriors which compliment the surrounding buildings and landscape. The interior design addresses a mix of open-plan workstations, teaming spaces and private offices.

4.9

4.9 Front elevation.
4.10 Site plan.

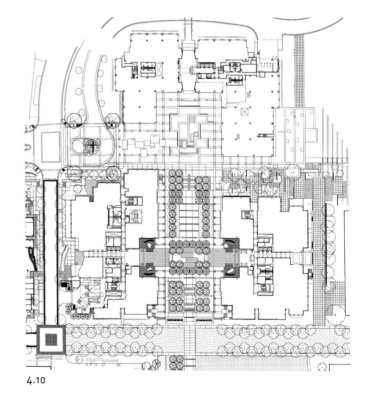

4.10

AMGEN, INC. BUILDING 38 │ THOUSAND OAKS, CALIF. │ 1999 │ 4.9, 4.10

SJ Yes. Both urban design and architecture rely on their ability to create physical form in space and time. However, urban design must be accessible or interpretable at some level by the widest possible audience. History suggests that great architecture, however, is frequently personal, intense, and sometimes even a conundrum in its own time, until later generations come to terms with the precocious nature of its vision. In reality, the great architect does not solve the problem. He invents a new problem, convinces the gatekeepers that this is a better problem, and then solves that in its place. He creates a metaphor of the problem, which he then solves metaphorically.

BF I am not sure today that a future generation will discover some great designer of our time who is unknown today. For sure, the research required for an urban design project attempts to define the problem, so we can come at it from a different angle. I suppose it's the nature of the problem being dealt with that makes the difference.

There is an interesting relationship between urban design and the notion of being deferential. For example, the creation of a conceptual structure inside which a lot of people can make decisions about the exact nature of land use—this is a goal in urban design. The way you structure a site plan to provide some further continuity to a city is important, and that translates into a whole series of restraints that are imposed for the common good. How relevant is that notion for architects, given the Nietzschean idea about form-making as a single project under the architect's absolute control? How do you reconcile that kind of project to provide order and continuity to the city? Is there any relevance to the idea of the role of an individual building in the larger urban scheme, at least for building designers? I suppose one possible answer is that architecture is informed by the city, not just in the sense of designing the building with a sense of context, but conveying the idea of the city today. The city is constantly changing. Los Angeles, for example, is amazing. I can't believe all the things that have happened in recent years. Many major corporations have left the city and no one seems to notice that they are gone! The gap is being filled by small businesses. The future of the city is being generated before our eyes. It's unbelievable, the resilience of this city. There are messages in that. And as architects and urban designers, we are trying to provide a kind of structure to encourage that kind of self-renovation.

149

4.11

4.12

4.11 Rear entrance
4.12 Ground floor gallery

SJ That's a way in which urban design and architecture may be very different. Urban design requires a kind of neutrality, a kind of systemic view or matrix that allows change to happen in the city, both the ones that are now and those unforeseen changes that will happen in the future. In architecture, on the other hand, neutrality may be exactly the opposite of what you want to achieve. You may want to create a physical metaphor of an idea, which is highly specific, and which confronts the city, and challenges the city to reform itself around it.

I do think, however, that the thing that joins us is that there is a desire to understand the big picture and the widest possible context, whatever the scale, whether it is an urban problem or architecture. We have an interest in understanding the forces, framing them and mending the tapestry with design, at the scale of the site, the neighborhood, the city or the world. It's the idea of connecting design to our value systems. That's what keeps us together I suppose .

BF Our urban design projects are anything but neutral. They are organized about armatures that keep them from becoming obsolete or insignificant. The value system is critical. We are always looking for systems, circumstances, and conditions that are going to inform us about what will happen in the future. The actual state of the city is, obviously, a way of informing urban design. A high level of awareness is an important commonality between our work in architecture and urban planning. What really differentiates architecture and urban design is the *degree of control.* As designers, how much control do we need to exercise over the product? The urban designer realizes that he can't control certain things, because there are so many different things happening, or so many possibilities. In fact you want to encourage the freedom for people to do things. It is about renewal. Certainly building designers—and this includes some of the best-known people—run into problems, because they develop systems that are so idiosyncratic that only they themselves can navigate within those systems. And for those systems to work in the real world would require a control mechanism, a highly centralized political system, which leads us to things we don't want to deal with. There is a kind of tyranny in this.

SJ Those architects would probably object to that observation, and might characterize their work as personal, humanist or perhaps socialist. But the last two decades have taught us, in a lot of ways, about the totalitarianism of the collective. Whether it's the

151

152

4.13 "In designing the Byron Winery, we thought of similarly tangible...metaphors, such as the beautiful folds in the rolling hills in norther Santa Barbara County."

BYRON WINERY | SANTA MARIA VALLEY, CALIF. | 1996 | FIGURES 4.13–4.18

4.14

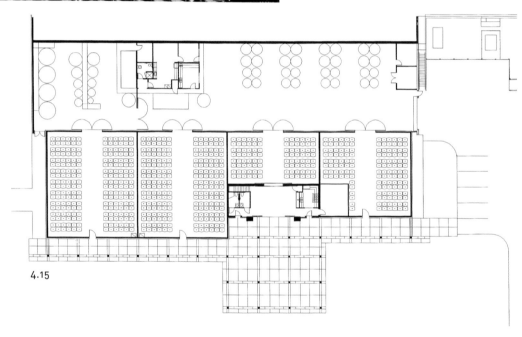

4.15

4.14 Model, bird's eye
perspective.
4.15 First-level plan.

absolute power of governments, global markets and advertising, the media, or cultural arbiters and brokers of specialized knowledge, the power, and even the political correctness of the collective can be as absolute as the power of the few.

And of course, issues of power bring us around to the "C" word: *control*. And I would suggest that the control thing is fundamental to the art of architecture.

Even though the notion of control in general is implicitly negative, I believe that for the architect it is the necessary link between vision, or idea, and realization. Control must be protected in order to ensure that the metaphoric life of the idea can be read in the text of the design.

BF Well, in urban design we draw upon metaphors continually. It's not necessarily in history that we look for metaphors, although we could find them. In reality, we use art. We look at paintings. We have done this, in fact, on a number of projects. In the case of the Indian Wells public park system we looked at the California *plein air* painters. While there is a literalism to their work, there is also an intangible quality that comes

155

across. We tried to emulate the way that those painters framed the inter-relationship of the sky, the mountains and the desert plain, and we tried to capture the spirit of those paintings in our public park system. So, in certain views of the parks, you can recall these elements. You don't see buildings because they are screened by earthen mounds. Instead, you see the desert plain, the mountain background and the sky. In a painting, you can understand those elements and translate them in a literal sense. In the plan, however, we are drawing upon abstraction—the land-scape scheme alludes to something else, to the natural landscape.

California Poppy Field

So this is an example of how we can draw upon abstraction and the metaphorical in plan making. I think that the grid itself uses abstraction as a basic structure. It is an abstraction, in one way, of infinite space, because it can go on forever in all four directions. But we do shape it and give it hierarchy by the way we distribute the activities that go on it.

SJ It gets back to that idea of the middle ground that we struggle with...

4.16 "...We thought of the roof form as something analagous to a musical structure...the curve of the Byron roof is in effect a simple harmonic chord, perhaps a major triad. And then the way it is pulled and pinched to create the porch, to bring light, to reveal spots of color, to expose structure..."

4.18 View into front entrance.

BYRON WINERY | SANTA MARIA VALLEY, CALIF. | 1996 | 4.16

BYRON WINERY | SANTA MARIA VALLEY, CALIF. | 1996 | 4.17

BYRON WINERY | SANTA MARIA VALLEY, CALIF. | 1996 | 4.18

BF ...because I think the idea of metaphor is itself an abstraction...

SJ ...right, because all language is abstraction. And we're back to the relativity, or undecidability, of language again. As mentioned, the urban designers have focused on California *plein air* painting as a metaphor, in effect, for visually organizing an approach, in this case, to a desert master plan for Indian Wells. This is, I believe, a very physical and tangible metaphor of certain artists' vision of color, sky, and landscape in California, and, interestingly enough, a particular sense of the balance between abstraction and literal representation in painting. At some level, I believe this metaphor when used in urban design has become a culturally absorbed image and can now function as a tool in building community consensus for a particular design scheme.

In designing the Byron Winery, we thought of similarly tangible and frankly, obvious, metaphors, such as the beautiful folds of rolling hills in northern Santa Barbara County. But on other levels, we thought of the roof form as something analogous to a musical structure. In jazz, a chord, for example, has an overall shape, something referred to as a "stack". This stack is a collection of tones from top to bottom that define its complexity. The curve of the Byron roof is in effect a simple harmonic chord, perhaps a major triad. And then the way it is pulled and pinched to create the porch, to bring in light, to reveal spots of color, to expose understructure. These are the harmonic extensions or dissonances in the stack, which give the chord complexity, depth, and specificity. These layers make something both simple and visually digestible, and yet worthy of more attention.

BF Research helps us to understand a place through its history. Also, we look for clues to less tangible issues in art. And we look to universal models of organizing and structuring space. Sacramento's East End began with a study of Sutter's plan for the city and how public parks evolved in the heart of the Capitol. That is why we decided to let the Capitol Park evolve by extending it into the project. At the San Francisco Piers, developing a new pier addition to mend the interrupted rythm of the piers along the Embarcadero seemed appropriate. A straightforward reference to the bulkhead, "finger" pier, and pavilion in the new YMCA building establishes the deep structure within which an interesting architecture can make sense and be acceptable to a larger public. In the Native American project, a different set of references to the inseparable nature of building and earth similarly establishes the deep structure.

159

| HIGHWAY 111 SPECIFIC PLAN | INDIAN WELLS, CALIF. | 1988 | FIGURES 4.19–4.26 |

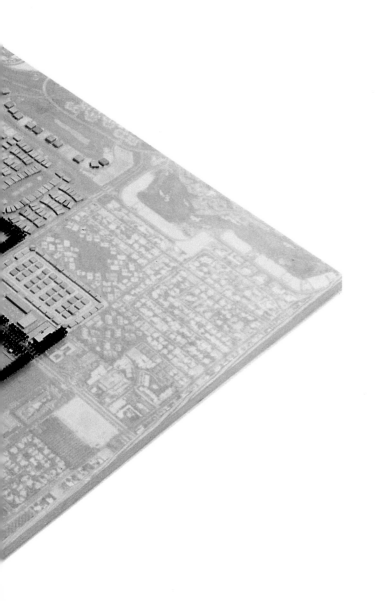

4.19 The scheme for the urban design of a 3.5-mile highway corridor that traverses this desert resort community. The plan recommends land uses, circulation improvements and landscape features to be implemented via a Specific Plan. The project provided an opportunity to guide development consistent with the physical heritage of the town, recapture natural elements of the desert landscape within the town boundaries and augment the public realm with cultural and civic institutions, while providing a realistic plan for future development.

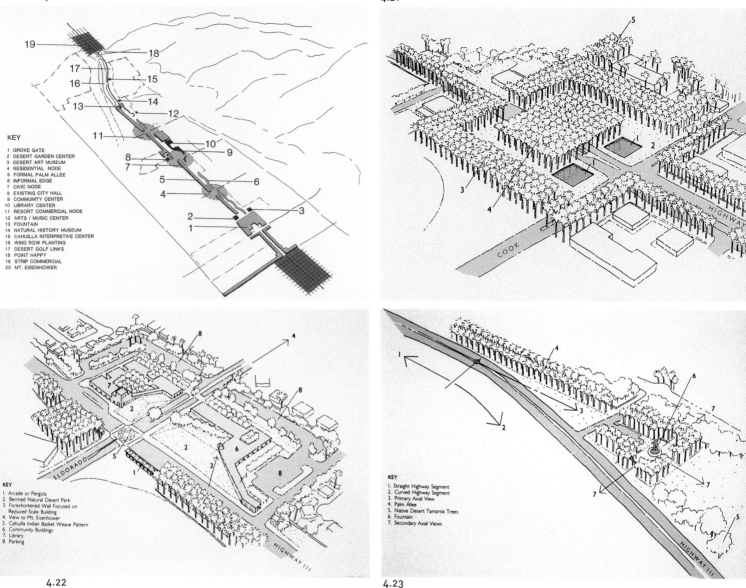

4.20

KEY
1 GROVE GATE
2 DESERT GARDEN CENTER
3 DESERT ART MUSEUM
4 RESIDENTIAL NODE
5 FORMAL PALM ALLEE
6 INFORMAL EDGE
7 CIVIC NODE
8 EXISTING CITY HALL
9 COMMUNITY CENTER
10 LIBRARY CENTER
11 RESORT COMMERCIAL NODE
12 ARTS / MUSIC CENTER
13 FOUNTAIN
14 NATURAL HISTORY MUSEUM
15 CAHUILLA INTERPRETIVE CENTER
16 WIND ROW PLANTING
17 DESERT GOLF LINKS
18 POINT HAPPY
19 STRIP COMMERCIAL
20 MT. EISENHOWER

4.21

COOK

HIGHWAY I

4.22

ELDORADO

HIGHWAY 111

KEY
1. Arcade or Pergola
2. Bermed Natural Desert Park
3. Foreshortened Wall Focused on
   Reduced Scale Building
4. View to Mt. Eisenhower
5. Cahuilla Indian Basket Weave Pattern
6. Community Buildings
7. Library
8. Parking

4.23

HIGHWAY 111

KEY
1. Straight Highway Segment
2. Curved Highway Segment
3. Primary Axial View
4. Palm Allee
5. Native Desert Tamarisk Trees
6. Fountain
7. Secondary Axial Views

4.24 "...We have focussed on California plen air painitng as a metaphor...a cery physical and tangible metaphor of certain artists' vision of color, sky and landscape...

"You don't see buildings because they are screened by earthen mounds. Instead, you see the desert plain, the mountain background and the sky."

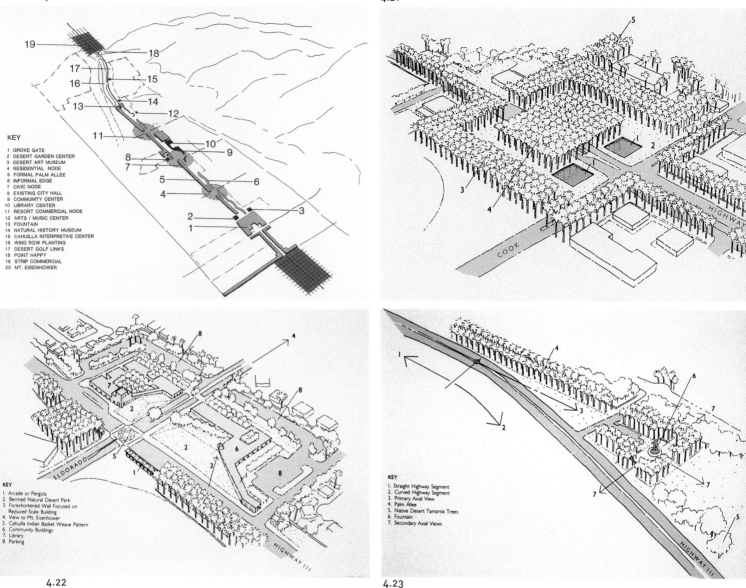

HIGHWAY 111 SPECIFIC PLAN | INDIAN WELLS, CALIF. | 1988 | 4.20–4.23

SJ There are limitations to research, however. Research may elicit some powerful idea or promote a particular position, but those in themselves are not physical design solutions.

BF True. Research offers us a method for discovery, of tracking the memory of a place. I think the things we look for are oftentimes abstractions that have to be translated.

SJ My observation is that in urban design, most of the research is focused on understanding the sense of the preexisting place…

BF …and, more. History is only part of the search. One looks to the city, the context and beyond for meaning.

163

SJ Whatever our differences, and clearly there are some, there are important commonalities. Urban design is about physicality. And, of course, architecture is about physicality. We have talked a lot about metaphors, and how physical work can resonate with other endeavors and other systems of thought. Still, having said all that, I believe—apparently more than Bill—that each medium must succeed or fail within the universe of that medium. While a work of dance can gain much as a collaboration with, for example, cinematography and poetry, the essential structure of dance is about the human form and its movement in space. These various collaborations must inform or support that essential experience in some new way for it to be great dance.

BF I see the craft of architecture as being inseparable from the city or some of the other issues that you talk about. In the process of design, one goes from conceptual, broader, and comprehensive issues to specific issues, having to do with the construction of the buildings. Usually, urban design comes first and building design comes later on. In a perfect world, the process is seamless between the two. It's a kind of interesting dialectic. The result has been that some projects are more interrelated than they might have been without that collaboration.

164

4.24 "We tried to emulate the way...painters framed the interrelationship of the sky, the mountains and desert plain, and we tried to capture the spirit of those painting in our public park system."

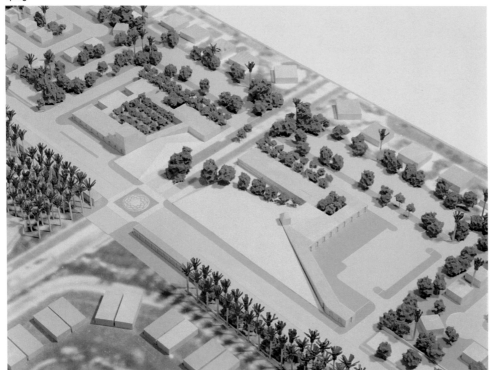

HIGHWAY 111 SPECIFIC PLAN │ INDIAN WELLS, CALIF. │ 1988 │ 4.25–4.27

SJ These are projects with many moving parts. And we need the contributions of many talented people. Also, in some cases, these projects begin as a programming or master planning, or even a site selection, effort. Architecture may be way down the line.

BF The logic expressed in our search for meaning, plus a mature intuition about a wide range of design experiences, can only expand and enrich the collaboration between architecture and urban design. The art of what we do relies on this rich matrix. Witness the broad range of buildings and urban design projects we have been able to attract. The potential is significant.

SJ It seems to me that the simplest way to understand this relationship is that there are two orbits that share an area of overlap. It is fortunate and productive that we know each other's orbit and we generally agree on the overlap. The unusual strength of this arrangement, which we were alluding to earlier, is that each discipline operates fully and forcefully in its own universe, and when there's an overlap we can provide a bridge that most design studios cannot. And, from the perspective of our overall practice, we are never in a position to be tempted to sell a weak discipline in order to get work in a strong one.

167

BF Strength is in a unified office and the future involves collaboration.

SJ I think we have probably said this before, but I want to return this conversation to the more general condition of the day. First, we've talked about global trends, advertising, media, big architecture, urban design, and all the rest. But as projects of increased scale and interconnectivity cohere around various assumed universal truths, or solutions, or points of view, we must create space for the individual, for the individual voice. In a way, it's all about finding one's own voice, and we should be creating policies, plans, and architecture that support that search. Second, we should not abandon, in this highly intellectualized life we all live, our bodies and the natural world around us. As inhabitants, we are physical beings, and as professionals, we are designers of physical space against the vast backdrop of nature. Whatever else design comes to mean, we want to experience it physically, firsthand and beyond metaphor.

CENTERING, FRAGMENTS, and the DEFINITION of PLACE

BILL FAIN I would like to talk about the concept of *centering*. In the design process, centering is a way to focus or give order and structure to space by establishing a strong sense of identity and place. Even in cases in which designers use similar structures in different places, these structures can be "regionalized" by adapting them to local conditions. The idea of centering challenges global tech culture, which promotes the notion of generalized space, which is everywhere and nowhere at the same time. At its best, centering is an approach that draws from local conditions—history, culture, geography, the ecology of the place—to determine the character of space, while relying upon what we have called deep structure for its order and orientation. Now, centering does not always mean making a center in a literal sense. Instead, it is about coming up with a unique identity for a place, whether it is the Central Business District of Beijing or the Amgen campus in Thousand Oaks.

At Amgen, centering is a straightforward idea. The original industrial park was never conceived as a unified campus. Parcels were laid out along a suburban road and buildings were developed on those parcels for individual owners. Amgen's first building was among them. Over the ensuing years Amgen acquired all 50 or so parcels. The issue then was how do you bring order to this place—or better, how do you create a center that brings these diverse buildings and sites into the whole? We cut a series of open spaces into the existing industrial park—it's like we inserted them surgically— including a north-south terrace intersected by an east-west paseo—a tree-lined walking street—and at the crossing we placed a central park that centers the entire campus. Those spaces give the campus the sense of being finite and defined. It is a solution that is unique for that place alone. A sustainable landscape with a characteristically California flavor supports the informal culture of the institution.

SCOTT JOHNSON I think the word "center" is attractive because it describes the goal without fixing the methodology or the tools necessary to create a center where one did not previously exist.

| AMGEN, INC. MASTERPLAN | THOUSAND OAKS, CALIF. | 1995 | FIGURES 5.1–5.3 |

172

5.1 In addition to the design of major new buildings, Johnson Fain has designed numerous site improvements within Amgen's 120-acre master plan that create a highly organized and identifiable center from what began as poorly-related buildings in a typical industrial park. These include: an enhanced main entry gateway; new open space and view corridors; revised internal vehicular and service drives; creation of new courts, terraces, plazas and landscape opportunities as well as a coherent site-wide network of pedestrian *paseos*.

5.2 Existing site

5.3 Master plan improvements

5.3

BF At the same time, the idea of centering is not simply replicating so-called "town centers," using developer terminology. In Irvine, the city came to realize that it did not have a downtown. If someone asked where downtown Irvine was, nobody had an answer. So they did a study of the area in an attempt to determine how to make a downtown. The problem with the idea was that the deep structure, the urban model, was flawed.

SJ The "vessels" of urbanism.

BF They tried to create a "there" there for Irvine, but the whole thing died in frustration, because they could never figure out how to create the kind of city context that people could relate to. They had all these very large sites and projects, each of which was self-contained, inaccessible by foot, and structured for the scale of the car. Worse, each building was centered around a plaza that had little or no relationship to the street. None of the proposed buildings supported a scale of development that could foster pedestrian activity and mixed-use development of an urban kind.

SJ What happened in Irvine is a very common problem. The impulse to create a center is good, but people get themselves locked into a set of priorities that do not promote urbanism and are difficult to overcome. In this case, the enormous scale of both the street pattern and the blocks, the huge tracts of parking which segregate land uses, and the failures to incorporate natural features and mixed-use zoning at the outset.

BF Centering can be achieved in other ways without literally framing a space with buildings. Centering can be something like a narrative. We referred to this earlier in our discussion of the Japanese garden. The plan for the garden at Shugakuin was less formal, even *deferential*. You discovered the center only after you had gone through a procession of spaces in the garden. You were not immediately aware of the center, you see, but discovered it later on. The actual center was deferential to a greater idea about the whole. Now, we can't follow the Japanese example, not in any literal way. Most of the master planning that we do has a Western European literalness to it. But there are European examples in older cities that are subtle and intriguing such as fractured or fragmented spaces which are quite different, for example, than the familiar typology of the centralized Italian piazza.

AMGEN, INC. BUILDING 30 | THOUSAND OAKS, CALIF. | 1998 | FIGURES 5.4–5.9

175

5.4 Building 30 is a 360,000 square foot research laboratory designed for Amgen, the bio-technology company. Planned in two phases and two buildings, the complex houses laboratories, offices and technical support spaces. Project requirements include interstitial service areas, clean rooms, NMR, cell-banking rooms and high-hazard areas. Labs are highly flexible, allowing for complete reconfig-uration of partitions to meet future needs. The facilities include a science conferencing center and a sky-lit pedestrian arcade linking the two structures.

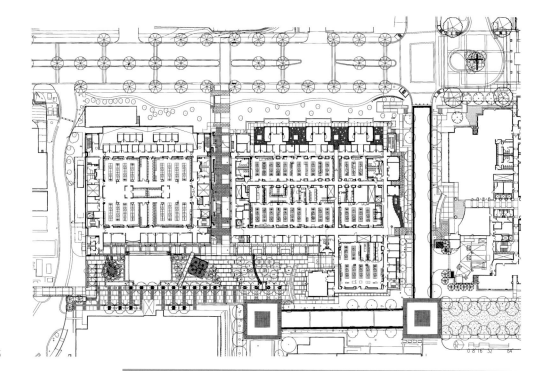

5.5

176

5.5 Ground floor plan
5.6 View of central garden

5.6

AMGEN, INC. BUILDING 30 | THOUSAND OAKS, CALIF. | 1998 | 5.2, 5.3

In Rome, one space that has interested me for years is Piazza in Campo Marzio. You really have to look for it. It's not easy to find, even though it is quite visible on the 1748 Nolli map of the city. It does not stand out like Piazza Navona or Campo de Fiori or other, more conventionally centered spaces. If you look at the fabric of Rome, many of these centered spaces seem to occur naturally because they all have a clearly identifiable purpose. Some spaces are gathering places, or places for interaction and socializing, and other spaces are ceremonial. Highly centered spaces of this kind are often very symmetrical and very legible.

Piazza in Campo Marzio is a different kind of space. It is less centered and more fragmented. It is squeezed at its center on two sides—the space looks like a bow tie in plan—and the two spaces that result make reference to the streets beyond the piazza. So this kind a space is a departure from the traditional idea of a center. This kind of space is almost never talked about. It's not in any of the literature. It is a transitional space there where a number of very old Roman roads converge. It may have been quite different at one time. During the Renaissance, and maybe slightly earlier, there were several *palazzos* built along the piazza. Now, these *palazzos* were not grand palaces like the Palazzo Farnese. They were smaller buildings, perhaps intended for the merchant class. My guess is that Piazza Marzio started out as a larger space formed by the crossroads. At some point, however, the palazzos were enlarged and began to encroach on the piazza, so that the shape of the space became more defined by the irregular edge of the buildings than by the meeting of the different roads. The space is kind of a no-place space. Instead of being regular in form, it is very irregular and fragmented, like a Brownian movement in the city. That kind of space interests me. There are many of these places that we don't even recognize because we have become so accustomed to them. But the idea of a fragmented space is a useful one in urban design, because these spaces give character to a city.

Since we are on the topic of Rome, I would like to mention the Tiber River Study. It proposes to create new relationships between the city of Rome and the Tiber River and makes use of the notion of fragments. Here, we are forced to be fragmentary, because it would be impossible at this late date in history to impose a single, continuous edge or section along the banks of the Tiber, as was done in the 1870s. The city is too densely developed and there is too much going on. But we can introduce a number

177

AMGEN, INC. BUILDING 30 | THOUSAND OAKS, CALIF. | 1998 | 5.7

AMGEN, INC. BUILDING 30 | THOUSAND OAKS, CALIF. | 1998 | 5.8

180

of different "fixes" in different places. These fixes are fragments, insofar as they only work for small areas before being interrupted by something else. These fragments, however, also show something interesting about the fragment, which is that it alludes to a larger whole. The act of creating fragmentary connections between the city and the river alludes to the larger condition of the river running continuously through the city, as well as the intimate inter-relationship between the city and the river that has existed for thousands of years.

SJ We use fragmentation here in much of the architectural work, even though it is sometimes different from the kind of fragmentation you describe at the Piazza Marzio. While our Middle School in North Hollywood is very much a center for the students and the neighborhood community, it is not a center in a traditional, physical sense. What drives the design of the Middle School is a series of strands. The school is located right on Laurel Canyon Drive, one of a zillion endless boulevards in LA. In a sense, the plan of the school takes up the linear strip, or strand, of the boulevard and adds to that a series of built and implied strands which penetrate the depth of the site and make up the deep structure of the project. In your mind, you can imagine the strands vanishing off into the site and beyond, attempting to organize everything. Like the Piazza Marzio, it may have started out as a simple form, but then life happened and ate away at the edges, so what originally had been a clear and defined idea is now a kind of blur. There is a fuzzy ambiguity to the school building: Is it a center or is it a transitional place of movement? It hums somewhere in the middle.

181

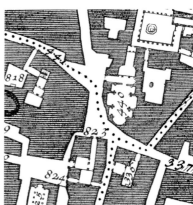
Piazza Marzio, Nolli Map

Similarly, the Piers project in San Francisco has something fragmentary about it. We introduced a dissonance, a kind of either/and condition, between this new structure and the existing piers. On one hand, it is one more "finger" pier like all the other piers along the Embarcadero. At the same time, it is not like other piers, because of its YMCA program (climbing wall, BMX arena, pool pavilion) and the struggle to make all these different things happen on the same pier. These forces complicate life and complicate the design as well. As architects, we can either force that complexity into some kind

TIBER RIVER STUDY | ROME, ITALY | 2002 | FIGURES 5.10–5.14

NEW PEDESTRIAN STAIRS
TO RIVER AND NEW BIKE RAMPS

PONTE ROTTO
RECONNECTS RIVER BANKS
AS A PEDESTRIAN BRIDGE

CAFÉS

FLOOD WALL AMPHITHEATER

CAFÉ
TIBER RIVER LOCK
ABOVE PONTE CESTIO

NEW "FLOOD GATES"
INSTALLED AT THE PIAZZA

A A

LANDSCAPED PARK &
PEDESTRIAN PROMENADE BUILT
ABOVE SUBTERRANEAN ROAD

REMOVE EXISTING PONTE PALATINO

NEW LOCATION FOR PONTE PALATINO
TO IMPROVE TRAFFIC CIRCULATION

OPEN THE RIVER WALL TO RECONNECT
THE TEMPLE OF VESTA AND THE
PIAZZA DELLA BOCCA DELLA VERITÀ

184

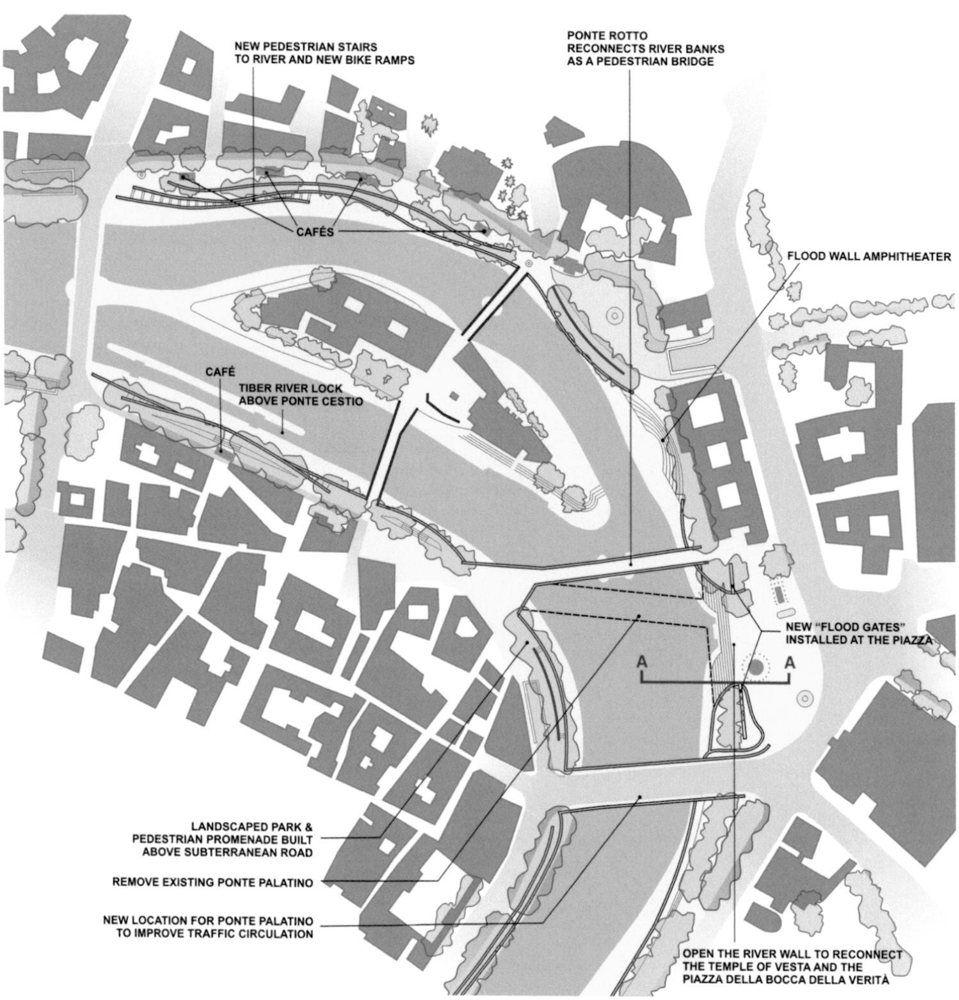

5.10 The Tiber River Study creates a vision for an active River Basin in which strategic modifications to the river-banks and walls can better connect the River to the everyday life of the City. This assumes an approach which is at times opportunistic in identifying potential River improvements and benefits, ranging from small-scale, incremental developments to aggressive, large-scale urban renewal projects. The Tiber River Study was completed under a Rome Prize Fellowship.

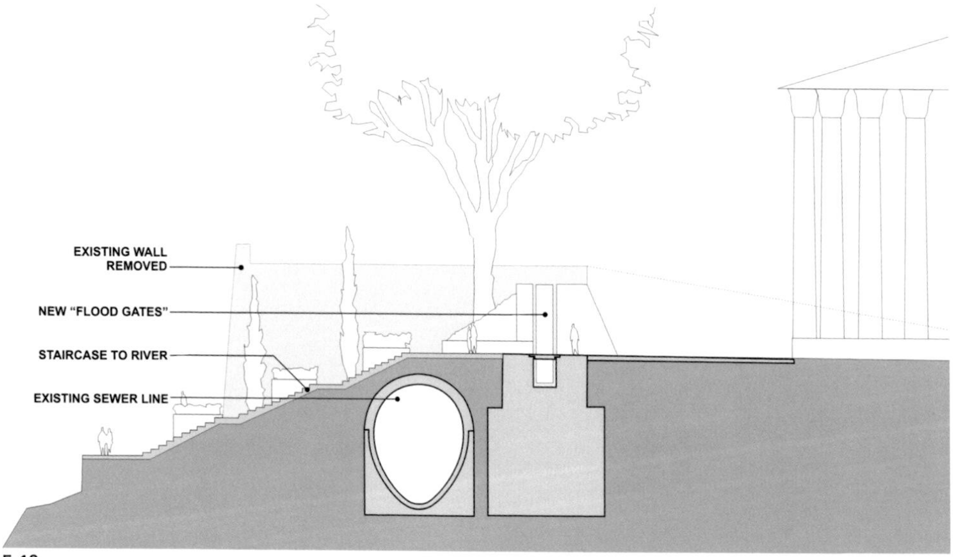

EXISTING WALL
REMOVED

NEW "FLOOD GATES"

STAIRCASE TO RIVER

EXISTING SEWER LINE

5.12

of pre-existing idealized form, or work with those forces and allow them to describe a new formal language through the struggle.

The use of fragments and their importance in design probably can't be overstated. Inevitably, and increasingly, we are confronted with both program elements which have no historic or natural conflation, as well as our own discovery as designers that only pieces, or fragments, are the available resources we have to approximate, or point to a central idea. They may be fragments of our own making, or, as in the case of Piazza Marzio, they may be historic fragments, traces of the past that we come upon when addressing design.

I am reminded here of the Nestlé USA Headquarters we designed several years ago. In that building, there was a fragment which was composed of a bay window, in effect, five stories high, and one column width wide. And that fragment was used over and over motivically, as in a fugue, cut here, lifted there, framed, unframed, more glass, less glass, etc. etc. Its repetition and recall suggested that it was part of an evolving universe of form generated by the fragment. It pointed toward something conceptual, and larger than itself. Constellation Place, the new tower in Century City, uses a three-story-high fragment and then staggers it on a shifting 10-foot grid to imply movement and create a third dimension in the wall. On a very different scale, the Gooden house in Malibu represents a collection of room fragments casually nested together against the curl of a hill. This is very much in evidence as you walk through the house or view it from below the hill. And it is apparent in the ground floor plan. Now that it's done, it reminds me in some ways of a village of fragments built over time, but in fact it's built all at one time in one house.

185

Nestlé USA Inc. Headquarters, Glendale, California

BF Staying with the idea of the fragment, if you were to separate the building from the earth mound at the Native American complex, the building would be revealed to be a highly fragmented piece of architecture and very different in character than when it is embedded in the earth.

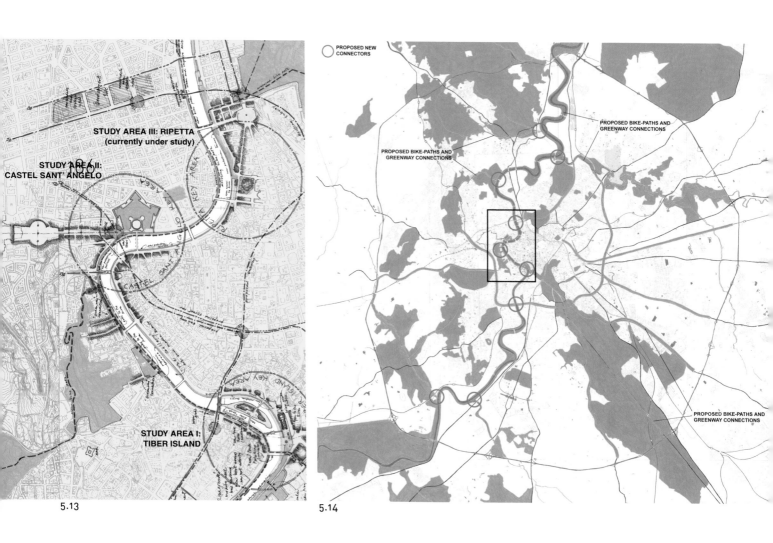

5.13 Tiber River study areas

5.14 Proposed regional open
space system

SJ It is an "open" system.

BF The architecture is completely dependent on another order, that is, on the larger landscape scheme.

SJ It would make no sense if you just took the architecture out of it; the two are co-dependent.

BF The entrance to the Native American complex is a series of fragments or arcs. Native Americans believe that life is circular—it's actually a spiral that is like a circle progressing through time. You come upon the same experiences again and again in life, but then again they are not the same, because you have progressed. That's why we use a spiral mound; it's a circle that progresses in time, like a coil from earth to heaven. The building intercepts this progression, as if it were one fragment in time in the course of that long progression. The center is defined by combining the building and earth.

LAUSD EAST VALLEY MIDDLE SCHOOL #1 | NORTH HOLLYWOOD | 2001 | FIGURES 5.15–5.19

5.15 East Valley Middle School is located on a 9.5 acre site in Los Angeles' San Fernando Valley to accommodate 1,600 students. Campus buildings are organized around a large public square that serves as the school's entry and major social center. The square is defined by four major building areas including a Classroom and Administration Wing, Multi-Purpose Building, Multi-Media Center and Gymnasium/Fitness Center.

5.16

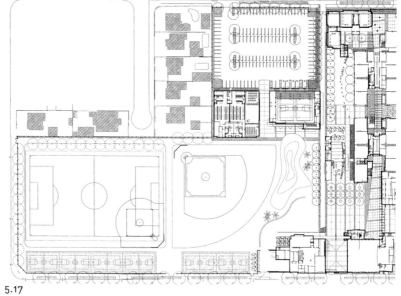

5.17

5.16 Entrance elevation
5.17 Site plan
5.18 Entrance

BUILDING for the PUBLIC LIFE

SCOTT JOHNSON Have you noticed the special attraction that LA represents for the British? Aside from the obvious fact that it's a hell of a lot warmer here, I think LA and London have certain similarities. Both cities were cobbled together from small towns and hamlets.

BILL FAIN Los Angeles is a spread-out city like London, as Rasmussen points out in the title of his book, *London: The Unique City*. L.A. epitomizes that, even though it was built up much later and more quickly than London. L.A. started out as a bunch of streetcar suburbs, and the city filled in between the towns, just as London did after the introduction of the railroad. Brits like Reyner Banham seem to love it here...

SJ ...and Hockney and Isherwood.

BF They have a kind of innate understanding of L.A. The big difference between L.A. and London is that the spaces are more suburban here, which is interesting, because the American idea of suburbia reflects the English cultural viewpoint. In the Anglo worldview, the city is evil, while the countryside is good. In England, the rich live in the country and the poor are left in the town. It's the opposite in France and continental cities, in general. Now, there are historical reasons why L.A. is a suburban place. It's a young city that depends on the car. Also, L.A. didn't experience the City Beautiful Movement of the 1800s and the creation of great parks and open spaces that came with it. Whereas other great American cities in the 19th century, like Chicago and Boston, took on a new sense of civic definition, and had the benefit of that 19th century structure. L.A. never had that experience. That is why park building

Griffith Park, Los Angeles

came to Los Angeles way too late. It is difficult to cite a great park in Los Angeles. Griffith Park is limited by its topography and its distance from the built-up part of the city. The result is that L.A. has very little open space. Only 4 percent of the city is park-land. It's a garden city with no garden, except in the private backyards of single-family

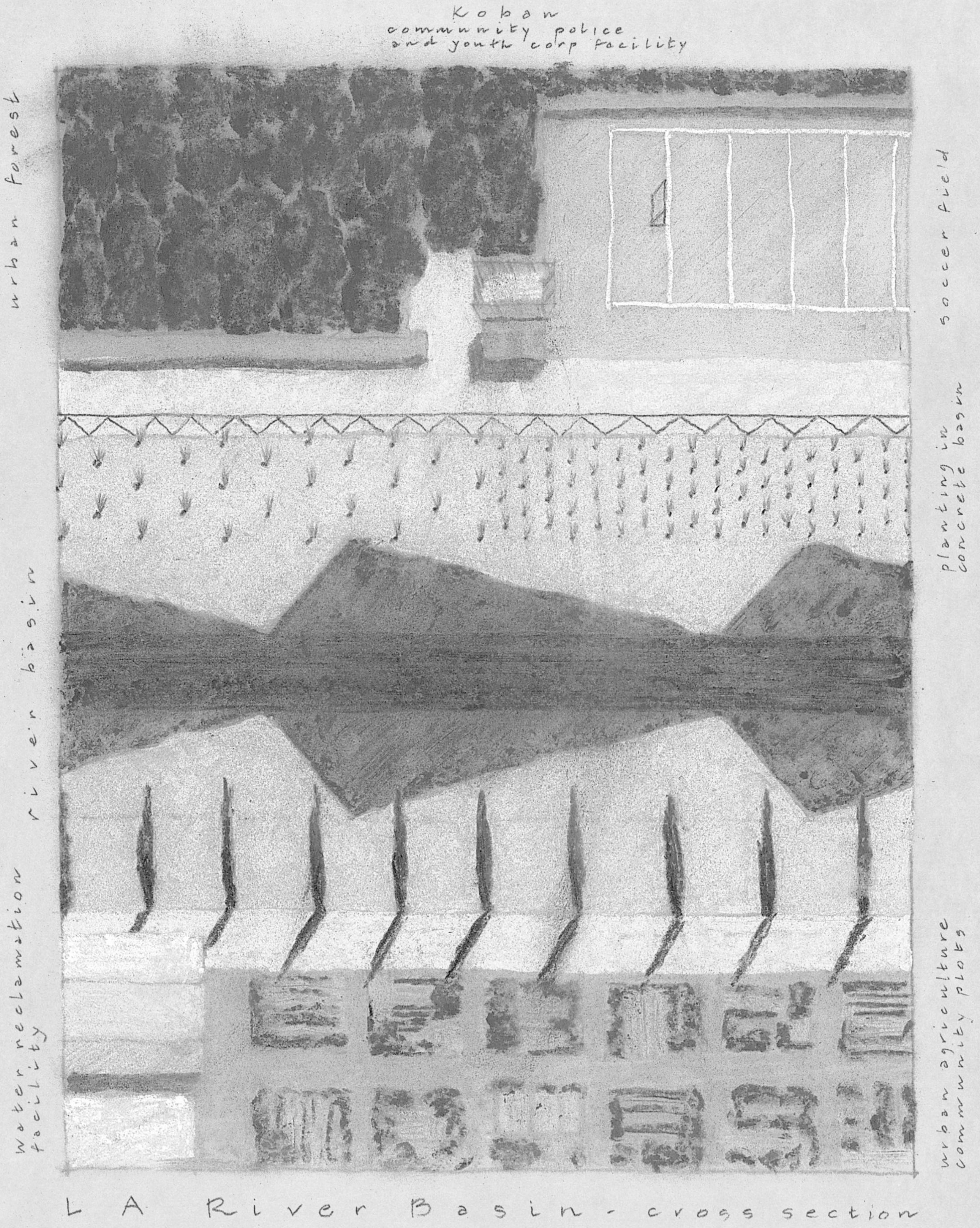

Koban
community police
and youth corp facility

urban forest

soccer field

planting in
concrete basin

river basin

water reclamation
facility

urban agriculture
community plots

L A River Basin - cross section

bikepath greenway

the beach

city high school
wall

elementary
school

fire station
and clinic

community park

multi family

| LOS ANGELES OPEN SPACE: A GREENWAYS PLAN | LOS ANGELES | 1994 | FIGURES 6.1–6.7 |

Converted Rail Right-of-way at
the Beach

6.3

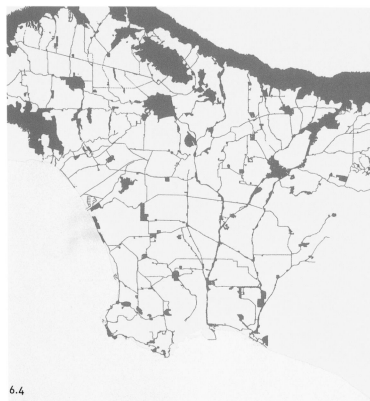

6.4

6.5

A Greenways Plan for Los
Angeles proposes the use of
readily available land resources
within existing infrastructure
systems to provide a significant
increase in public open space.
The plan views existing transit
lines, bikeways, rail right-of-
ways, rivers, flood control chan-
nels and power line easements
as elements in a county-wide
linear open space system. The
plan links the proposed open
space system to existing town
centers, schools, libraries, post
offices, and senior centers as
well as providing sites for new
facilities. The concept can be
the catalyst for establishing
additional public parks, squares
and plazas, thereby increasing
the amount of open space available for the use and enjoyment
of the public.

6.1 River section
6.2 Taylor Yard

6.3 Existing open spaces
6.4 Proposed greensway
6.5 Proposed developments
along greenways

detached dwellings. That's why in our Greenways project, we tried to find residual park space where it was available, and bring open space back to the city.

The logical areas to find new open space are publicly owned easements, like the land under utility lines, along rivers, and the abandoned red car right-of-ways. There is a lot of open space you drive by every day and never notice it. Ray Kappe said the Greenways project was trying to bring back the idea of the commons, that is, the areas in old cities where people were allowed to hunt and graze their cattle and so on. I don't think Ray was suggesting that people actually hunt in these places, but rather the idea that there would be a continuous edge of public green space throughout the city. He also remarked that the project was a kind way to reposition the city by introducing a network of open space that connects neighborhoods and organized development by locating new neighborhoods for an expanding city.

197

SJ Architects and planners here have been talking about this since the early 1930's, even though the idea of a commons is a throwback to the 19th Century, and earlier.

BF But the idea is having a hard time gaining official acceptance here, because of the intensely private, or even *privatistic* nature of Los Angeles. The city is laid out in a way that assumed that it would be forever suburban and forever dependent on the car. That means that it is hard to create urban amenities, because we do not have the density of development that supports the experiences we tend to think of as urban. When you are in London or Tokyo, you need only walk a few blocks to do all your shopping and get all your services, including transit. But in Los Angeles, even though it was put together from different hamlets, all those hamlets developed along traffic arterials that were designed for the car. There is no way you can walk to the next "village" in L.A. to find another set of village services; it would be like walking from Larchmont to Culver City or Little Tokyo. I think that Los Angeles exists on multiple scales, one scale for the car and another for the pedestrian. At one point, we determined that the distance you could cover in two minutes in the car was equal to about what you could do in 10 minutes on foot. So the spatial sense of L.A. is very different from places like San Francisco. Here, things are separated from one another. Our city is a very private city. And the civility of this city is questionable, as a result. I think it has a cultural impact. People are reluctant

6.6 Los Angeles River
at Griffith Park
6.7 Santa Monica Boulevard
at Century City

EXPERIAN CORPORATE HEADQUARTERS | COSTA MESA, CALIF. | 1999 | FIGURES 6.8–6.12

201

6.8 The Experian Corporate Headquarters is a new, low-rise office campus for an information-technology company that is designed to promote social interaction among employees. The four office buildings, main lobby and conference center are organized around a central landscaped courtyard and are linked by a system of arcades and canopy structures. Opportunities for social interaction are maximized by locating building elevators on the sides of the buildings facing the courtyard and conference center, and by providing wide stairs in support of a "walk-up" corporate culture. The courtyard is landscaped with a water feature, shade trees and outdoor social spaces. The interior design maximizes the open office environment at the perimeter of each floor, admitting natural light throughout.

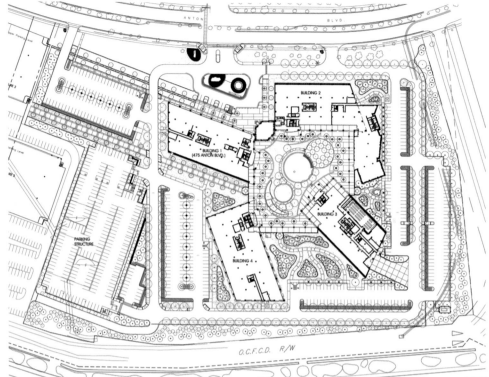

6.9

6.10

EXPERIAN CORPORATE HEADQUARTERS | COSTA MESA, CALIF. | 1999 | 6.9, 6.10

to commit to things; it's hard to get them to join up. The preference here is to stay in your own house, your own backyard, your own swimming pool. Perhaps there is something virtuous about that, at least in the Anglo sense. Social encounters for the most part do not take place in public. I was recently working on a project in Washington D.C. and there were some Los Angeles architects working down the hall. I saw more of them in Washington than I ever did in L.A.

SJ A number of years ago, after Joseph Giovannini had moved back to New York from Los Angeles, he wrote this great article about the differences between his experience in the two cities. He focused on how different his two morning trips to work turned out to be in each place. Each day in New York, he inevitably exchanged pleasantries with someone in the hall or elevator of his high-rise apartment building and acknowledged the presence of the doorman on his way out. On the sidewalk, he might recognize and say hello to a familiar face or two, stop at the corner to buy a paper from his usual vendor while scanning the magazine rack. Taking his paper, he would enter his favorite diner, for a quick breakfast, exchange a few words with the waiter across the counter, and perhaps recognize several diners on his same schedule. A word or two about headline news or sports, and he was on his way. Hello to the security guard in his office lobby, another hello to the receptionist on his floor, and he entered his work environment for the day.

But in Los Angeles, he had walked from the breakfast table of his single family house directly into the garage, entered his car, windows up, radio on and backed out onto the street with the help of an electronic garage-door opener. Fully encapsulated enroute to the office, he finally steered his car into his office garage, dove down to his basement parking stall, where he walked through a large concrete room inhabited by cars but no people, to the elevator, and with the press of a button, he appeared at his floor. He hadn't confronted a soul.

I may have missed a few details, but the difference between the two scenes couldn't be more striking. Our city has been organized for mobility and privacy at all costs. As a result, common social intercourse does not come easily here. Everyone knows that you can have privacy in New York City, but the constant public life you find yourself sharing requires you to develop a protocol for territories and appropriate

6.11

6.12

6.9 Experian site plan

6.10 Model

6.11 "The bottoms of the
buildings are accessible from
the park like quadrangle."

6.12 Conference center

behavior, whatever that happens to be. A common bond is forged, whether about intimacy, or frequently, about a kind of limited exchange. Still it exercises the community muscles and builds communication skills and strength. Los Angeles has been different. And this difference has been artfully chronicled in the works of Nathaniel West to early Joan Didion to the current writings of T. C. Boyle. Perhaps romanticized, but still all about the extreme fallout of privacy.

BF Absolutely. All this privacy affects our socialization. I think Scott mentioned New York and the importance of the sidewalk as an element in urban life. In Irvine, as in most new subdivisions, for example, there is a requirement to build curbs, gutters and sidewalks as in most new subdivisions, and there is an implicit urbanness in that an idea. On the other hand, if you go to Rancho Palos Verdes or Rolling Hills, the urban condition is what they term as semi-rural and there are no sidewalks. It's almost as if you had gone back to the past, where you got in your covered wagon to got around. If you see someone on the sidewalk here, it's almost as if something is wrong. People are not really supposed to be on the sidewalk. The sidewalk is seen as a place where problems happen in Los Angeles. It's a dirty place. It's stacks of old newspapers. It's for the homeless and the panhandlers. And that attitude gets reflected in the way we have designed our sidewalks. They're narrow and cramped. The street right-of way is about traffic and transportation, period. The upshot is that the use of the private car is maximized and glorified. That's where we are, like those great paintings of California roadways by Wayne Thiebaud.

205

SJ The sidewalk phenomenon that Bill is speaking about is like a scene from a Charlie Chaplin or Jaque Tati movie, depending on your sense of comedy. You can imagine the Little Tramp or Monsieur Hulot trying to walk sideways down an 18-inch sidewalk next to a roaring highway. His back is pressed against a tall building which vanishes up out of the frame. He is perspiring because there is no space to plant a shade tree and he can't breath amid the exhaust. Now, in order to move, he must squeeze by pedestrians, hydrants, and traffic signs on his narrow trail.

Charlie Chaplin in the film *Modern Times*

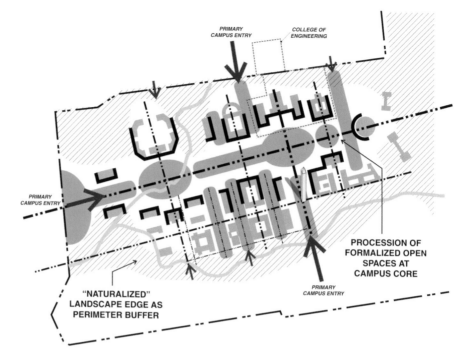

6.14

208

PRIMARY CAMPUS ENTRY

COLLEGE OF ENGINEERING

PRIMARY CAMPUS ENTRY

PROCESSION OF FORMALIZED OPEN SPACES AT CAMPUS CORE

"NATURALIZED" LANDSCAPE EDGE AS PERIMETER BUFFER

PRIMARY CAMPUS ENTRY

6.13–6.15 Davis Hall North includes 130,000 square feet of new laboratories, seminar rooms, state-of-the-art class-rooms, computing facilities and offices on the site of old Davis Hall at the University of California, Berkeley. The design, massing, and scale of the building respond to nearby Arts & Crafts buildings as well as the adjacent historic Naval Architecture Building. The project is a significant compo-nent of the new "Centers for Science and Innovation Program", a UC partnership of university, industry, and gov-ernment. Johnson Fain also completed a master plan for the College of Engineering that accommodates the requirements of inter-disciplinary curricula for both the College and the overall campus.

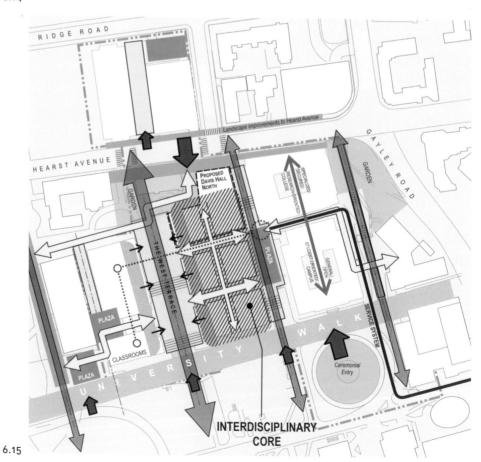

6.15

RIDGE ROAD

GAYLEY ROAD

Landscape improvements to Hearst Avenue

HEARST AVENUE

GARDEN

GARDEN

PROPOSED DAVIS HALL NORTH

SPECIALIZED/ SECURED/ RESEARCH-ORIENTED COLLEGE

STUDENT-ORIENTED CAMPUS

GENERAL OPEN

PLAZA

THE WEST TERRACE

PLAZA

CLASSROOMS

PLAZA

Ceremonial Entry

UNIVERSITY WALK

SERVICE SYSTEM

INTERDISCIPLINARY CORE

In fact, these conditions have become so poor and unacceptable that in recent years a number of forces have begun to coalesce around alternatives both in the inner city and in the suburbs. Suburban town center development has been an interesting movement to watch. It seems to represent a desire to recast the sense of a downtown, or community center, ready-made and from the ground up, much in the manner of suburban residential construction. We designed the first mixed-use buildings in the Valencia Town Center in Santa Clarita and while the first phases required courage and were slow to populate, the project is now quite built out and extremely well supported by the community there.

BF In a way, projects like the Valencia Town Center represent the triumph of an idea about the street and civility. But even though the project has a number of virtues, it is not perfect. You are seeing a single street that stands alone by itself. It is not organized spatially on a grid, like a traditional downtown. When the street begins to fill in and the urban energy starts to grow, there is no place for new merchants to go, at least the way it is set up right now.

209

SJ I would not put Valencia Town Center forward as a perfect example, but it is an example of the will and struggle for placemaking in traditional suburbia.

BF In some cases, in Santa Monica for instance, the regional mall gives birth to the shopping street, and then the shopping street becomes so successful that it causes the mall to be demolished. It's like the child going back and eating the father.

SJ Sounds like something out of Sir James Frazer.

BF I guess the real issue is, where is L.A. going? It seems to have turned some sort of corner, and entered a mid-life crisis.

SJ So much is going on right now. California is the world's fifth largest economy, and Los Angeles is the largest regional part of that. We're told that we're getting an additional 10 million immigrants statewide by 2025. Each year, we fail to meet our housing need

6.16, 6.17 Davis Hall, atrium space

UNIVERSITY OF CALIFORNIA BERKELEY DAVIS HALL │ BERKELEY, CALIF. │ 2001 │ 6.17

6.18 Model view of the new research center sited strategically between three existing historic buildings.

by an additional 10,000 units. A disproportionate amount of those new residents and that increasing need comes here. Then there are the related issues of schools, quality of life, transportation costs, and ultimately, the sustainability of all this. Solutions are being aggressively rethought or identified. One of those is the livability of the center city.

BF But here it is more challenging to live in the center city, because L.A. lacks a lot of the amenities of older cities. There is no great downtown park here, no pleasant shopping street, no beautiful Washington Square.

SJ That's true. Those urban energies have been sapped in the past.

213

BF At the same time, when people from Asia, who are accustomed to extreme residential densities, visit people who live in neighborhoods like Hancock Park, they are amazed, because people manage to live in the city and have a garden. It blows them away. But it would be simplistic to say that the only urban trend is "back to the city." We are also becoming more suburban, a trend which frankly being furthered by the internet. The question to ask is, What are the implications for the urban environment? There are all these forces at play that seem to tend away from urbanism and the idea of a center. The technology campus is a good example of that. Where is it taking us? I mean to say, where is it taking us in a tangible way, in terms of lifestyle? The culture of these organizations—the users of the technology campus—has become much less formal than a few years ago, and that informality has led to an environment where the relationship of home to work has become blurred so in essence the environment of the campus is an extension of the home, and to that extent provisions of the home have to be incorpo-rated within the campus. If Mom and Dad are spending more than eight hours a day in this environment, or actually staying home and working there is a kind of correlation between the two. Which leads to an idea about distance and space, it says that the commuting time between campus and home has to become less; ironically on the other hand, it can also be greater, because of technology, so there is kind of a dichotomy there.

The technology campus has also taught us that even though technology allows for greater decentralization, human interaction is paramount and the culture of these

CONSTELLATION PLACE | CENTURY CITY, CALIF. | 1999 | FIGURES 6.19–6.23

215

6.19 Constellation Place is the first high-rise office building to be built in Los Angeles in over a decade. The major tenant in the building is entertainment giant, Metro-Goldwyn-Mayer. Situated on six acres at the corner of Constellation Boulevard and Century Park West in a highly visible position in Century City, shopping, restaurants, entertainment and hotels contribute to this mixed-use neighborhood. The project provides 700,000 square feet of office space and a stand-alone parking structure for 2,800 cars. The building's exterior is designed with a highly faceted glass wall while the ground level and public spaces are tailored in natural stones and wood millwork.

216

campuses must encourage informal meetings to promote creative thinking. So the need for people to be next to each other has to occur. Not all communication can happen on the computer.

John Cleese

SJ John Cleese from the old Monty Python troupe is quite scholarly about this and gives lectures these days on the topic of creativity. It is interesting here that one of the studies he cites concerns architects, among others, and how some of the most creative architects appear to have built a relationship between productivity and the activity of play. Their conception of what they do is seen as playing, and in turn, this engagement seems to fuel their high levels of output. In this town, where producers yell out, "Get some talent in here!" or economists refer to most of us as "producers of intellectual content 'or' service providers", there is a very strong need to create an informal, fun, and relaxed working environment. There is also the need to create an environment where all the various parts of a complex lifestyle are accommodated and nurtured. Employees at Amgen, or NASA's Jet Propulsion Laboratory, for that matter, can bring their kids to work, drop them off at childcare, visit them during the day, go for a workout, eat what, when, and where they wish, work collectively when and where they schedule meetings, indoors or outdoors, or work privately, when they wish. As a whole, these are highly educated individuals whose contribution to their institution and to the quality of life for us all is very much tied to their ability to create. And so the design of their work environments is an important charge.

BF These environments are a way of life. The issue becomes, what are the implications of these islands of technology and business, whether Amgen or JPL or UC Berkeley or Genentech? How are they changing our cities? Are they an indicator of the future? Scott mentioned the ideas of fun and informality. In many ways, our more traditional U.S. cities, which are organized around formal structures, are becoming adaptively reused, being designed as more fun places to live, accommodating a variety of people, and taking on different meaning as a result. For example, downtown Los Angeles is becoming more of a residential neighborhood, not strictly an office environment in the central city. When people live here and occupy some of the spaces in these big buildings, they bring informality and complexity to this traditional business environment.

218

6.21 Elevator lobby

6.22 Ground floor entrance lobby

6.23 Entry to the base
of the new highly faceted
hi-rise tower.

CONSTELLATION PLACE | CENTURY CITY, CALIF. | 1999 | 6.23

SJ It's interesting to look back historically on how technology companies originally built their campuses and how they have defined the relationship between their community and the city. In the first wave of development in a place like California you would go out where land was cheap, where building constraints were few and you could nestle facilities together, and where you thought you would have the ability to grow. At Amgen, for example, they did what any smart guys would do. They went out to the edge of the county, bought up a bunch of land near their existing cheap space, took it down, and began to expand and plan. As they prospered, so did their city, and the increasing number of homeowners in the area, much as a result of their own growth. Pretty soon we have a more mature city, with a self image, a political structure, development regulations, and we still have Amgen, who is now bigger, more successful, and more international than ever before. And we have a need to mediate what Bill earlier referred to as Pareto-optimal solutions for both parties.

221

There are many different examples of this relationship between the technology campus and the city, and each is different in important ways. We have Silicon Valley in the Bay Area and the extraordinary damage done to the region due to a legacy of unfortunate land use planning. Next door we have the City of San Jose and its Redevelopment Agency struggling mightily to control and conduit the forces of growth to fit their vision of a pedestrian friendly garden city with considerable historic qualities. There's San Francisco, and the unique opportunity that we have had in setting the stage for further technology growth in Mission Bay. And there's Berkeley, the East Bay, north San Diego County, and Orange County, where we created the Experian Headquarters campus.

BF How do we adapt these existing cities to this new technology? What happens to the fringe areas, for example? Do they continue to grow, because people can live and work at home, and suburbia continues to spread, because people no longer need to work in the traditional work environment? That actually is not a positive, in environmental terms, because the urban areas continue to proliferate endlessly. On the other hand, we are getting to the limits of suburbia, because distances between the suburbs and job centers are getting too long, and it is difficult to get back into town for the job. The commute has become impossible.

PACIFIC CORPORATE TOWERS | EL SEGUNDO, CALIF. | 1999 | FIGURES 6.23–6.27

223

6.24 Pacific Corporate Towers is a comprehensive program of upgrades and design renovations to update the three-building, 1.6 million-square-foot complex, adapt its 1970's-era structures to the contemporary market and enhance its public spaces. The design includes new signage, lighting, landscape and architecture. An existing triangular courtyard was enclosed on the side facing the ocean with a transparent "windwall" of sloped glass and steel to deflect strong coastal wind.

Interior lobbies include marble floors, natural plaster, and milled wood and chrome walls. Extensive use of frameless glass and new landscaping maximize natural light and create a visual connection to the outdoors.

6.25 Ground floor lobby interior

SJ We may have reached our practical boundaries. Commute time. Cost of suburban infrastructure. And in California, significant reductions in arable land. Hopefully, further growth will take place in a more compact form.

BF Portland was the city that actually created growth boundaries, so the implication is the population still grows and it has to do it within predetermined boundaries so growth becomes more organized.

SJ So you can control and channel growth in that way...

BF ...yes, so the government can create boundaries. It's an idea about limits, about nature vs. urban development, and it's very political. More importantly, there is the notion of transportation, especially getting from one area to another that does not require the car. In the case of Portland, growth is predicated on the idea of expanding villages outside the growth boundaries of the city that are connected by public transit.

225

SJ A lot of the emigration from the city center has been generated by the availability of cheaper housing in the fringe areas. And there is the relative quality of schools, access to safe open space and recreation, adequate shopping and entertainment, etc. We struggle with all these issues in building up downtown L.A.. Markets allowing, one can build luxury highrise housing, or student housing, or even the occasional SRO, but the challenge is to provide both affordable and market-rate housing together. In the end, the diverse, fun, round-the-clock city center we're all trying for will include a mix of income groups and demographics.

BF A project like the Metropolitan Lofts, which incorporates loft housing and new construction, may be one answer.

SJ Yes, there is also the question of scale, of mediating the street scale of the city with the frequent high-rise scale of certain buildings. On Madison Avenue through Lower Manhattan, there is a comfortable ground level scale to the buildings because of their retail use, the architectural character of the bottom floors, and the permeability and

6.26 Ground floor lobby interior

size of tenant spaces along the sidewalk, despite the existence of tall buildings above. However as you enter the west 50's, buildings designed and built in the 70s and 80s shoot out of the ground at a completely different scale and deny the intimacy of the sidewalk.

Several of our recent high-rise towers have been built in Century City in West Los Angeles, and this neighborhood projects a very different sense of what a city might be. Additionally, each tower, although only one block away from the next, finds itself in a very different relationship with the public right of way. Still, each tower has to work at several scales at the same time. Like a movie starlet, the building gets a close-up: the entry, the base of the building, where you can get up-close and personal. The middle distance, where you make out the dress and articulation of the vertical aspects of the building. And the long view, or skyline shot, where the building resolves vertically and the character of the place is somehow transmitted to the widest possible audience. In each case, however, we try to be explicit about the way in which the building speaks to the urban grid.

BF That's a challenge, because the master plan of Century City, a 1960s scheme of point towers and plazas, is working against us.

SJ It's true. A point tower typically makes very little acknowledgement of its context. Additionally, the nature of the grid allows for superblocks that result in very undefined outdoor space. Finally, in all their exuberance, many of the other buildings in the area experiment with a kind of disorientation, which I, personally, don't find worth the effort. Shifted axes, squares rotated to 45 degrees, triangulation, etc.

So we try, among other things, to define our locations with these buildings. Twentieth Century Fox Plaza is perhaps the most iconic for while it's highly sculpted, the four sides of its square plan are identical and it is sited directly on axis with Olympic Boulevard to the west. SunAmerica Center is a tower whose primary entrance has a 45-degree orientation to the corner on which it sits. Pedestrians cross the street and enter here. And the large descending paraboloid that defines the entire building is generated from this siting. Finally, at the MGM Tower, our latest building, the floor plate is a modified rectangle that parallels the street, accepts pedestrian traffic on a diagonal bias, and this diagonal is motivic throughout the skin of the building.

227

6.27 New garden pyramid
against the backdrop
of an existing office tower.

It is our attempt to avoid the normal static properties of high-rise buildings, and imply movement, depth and transparency.

BF Century City was a 60s idea involving tall buildings on very large land assemblages. Downtown Los Angeles suffers from the same thing. It is the old urban renewal approach to revitalizing urban areas. Unfortunately, the result has been to build "big architecture" instead of creating a humane urban context.

In the building Scott mentioned, we have tried to give our buildings some kind of contextual meaning, by making the buildings respond appropriately to the place in which they reside, a stand alone building, a corner building, and a mid-block building That's how we explain it urbanistically. Each building treats the sidewalk as a conduit, as an extension of the building plan. Plus, each building relates explicitly to the street spatially. I think the character of Century City would have been better if all the buildings had been required to respect the street.

There is a whole discussion about modernism, really about modernist spatial ideas, such as Le Corbusier's notorious Voisin plan for Paris. The modernist city has been far less successful than the 19th century grid city. As we mentioned earlier, you can build a 20th century building within a 19th century grid, but the large, 20th century grid, such as the one at Century City, is far less versatile. The idea is to encourage choice and the ability to do buildings of many sizes, including smaller buildings. The city is a place that is basically out of control, in a strict sense of controlling all the design decisions. The art is to create a set of rules that encourage good buildings, or at very least does not prevent them from coming into being in the first place.

SJ It's interesting to talk about modernism from this perspective. Clearly our buildings represent a modernist aesthetic. But in their relationship to the urban environment, they are very far from being pure objects in a sea of universal space. I believe that life is more complicated than that now.

It's also interesting to see young architects take up their own interest in the modern movement. The new generation was not around in the1950s and 60s, and that legacy today offers us either a romantic artifact, or a way to clear the decks from the present and pick up modernism as a place to start fresh. In either case, the world has moved on, and it will be good to see how young architects address the shortcomings of their fathers.

229

AWARDS

2003
National AIA
Honors Award for Regional and Urban Design
Mission Bay
San Francisco, California

California Construction Link
Best of California Award
Constellation Place
Century City, California

Los Angeles Business Journal
Best Architectural Design
Constellation Place
Los Angeles, California

Building Design & Construction
Building Team of the Year, Award of Merit
Capitol Area East End Complex Block 225
Sacramento, California

Golden Nugget Award
Best Office/Professional Building
+ 60,000 square feet
Capitol Area East End Complex
Sacramento, California

Golden Nugget Award
Sustainable Non-residential Project
Capitol Area East End Complex
Sacramento, California

First Prize in Design Competition
Guangzhou Development Area Master Plan
Guangzhou, China

2002
Best of California Award
Sacramento Valley / Mixed-Use
Capitol Area East End Complex
Sacramento, California

Gold Nugget Award of Merit
Custom Home
Larchmont Residence
Los Angeles, California

First Prize in Design Competition
Beijing Zhongguancun International School
Beijing, China

First Prize in Design Competition
International Financial Resources Center
Beijing, China

First Prize in Design Competition
Master Plan and Key Area Urban Design
Jiangwan New Town
Shanghai, China

First Prize in Design Competition
Fangshan University Town
Beijing, China

2001
California Construction Link
Best of California Award
Capitol Area East End Complex
Sacramento, California

Building Owners and Management Association
International TOBY Award
500,000 to 1 million square feet
SunAmerica Center
Century City, California

First Prize in Design Competition
New Central Business District (CBD)
Beijing, China

2000
Gold Nugget Award of Merit
Rehabilitation
Junipero Serra Building
Los Angeles, California

Los Angeles Conservancy
Preservation Award
Junipero Serra Building
Los Angeles, California

California Preservation Foundation
Preservation Design Award
Junipero Serra Building
Los Angeles, California

1999
Southern California Development Forum
Outstanding Achievement Award
Junipero Serra Building
Los Angeles, California

Gold Nugget Award of Merit
Specialty Buildings
Queensway Bay Parking Structure
Long Beach, California

West Los Angeles Chamber of Commerce
Beautification Award
Queensway Bay Parking Structure
Long Beach, California

Building Owners and Management Association
Building of the Year
500,000 to 1 million square feet
Fox Plaza
Century City, California

1998
Los Angeles Chapter AIA
Design Award
Queensway Bay Parking Structure
Long Beach, California

California Council AIA
Award of Merit
Byron Winery
Santa Maria Valley, California

Building Owners and Management Association
Best Corporate Facility
Toyota Motor Sales Headquarters
Torrance, California

Building Owners and Management Association
Best Building - 250,000 to 500,000 square feet
Pasadena Towers
Pasadena, California

1997
Gold Nugget Award of Merit
Public/Private Special Use Facility
Byron Winery
Santa Maria Valley, California

Gold Nugget Award of Merit
Office/Professional Buildings
Los Angeles Area Chamber of Commerce
Los Angeles, California

Gold Nugget Award of Merit
Custom Home
Johnson/Bates Residence
St. Helena, California

Los Angeles Chapter AIA
Design Award
Los Angeles Civic Center
Shared Facilities and Enhancement Plan
Los Angeles, California

Los Angeles Business Council
Beautification Award
Los Angeles Civic Center
Shared Facilities and Enhancement Plan
Los Angeles, California

1996
Los Angeles Business Council
Urban Beautification Award
New Commercial Mid-Rise
Warner Bros. Bridge Building
Burbank, California

1995
Building Owners and Management Association
Best Rehabilitation and Modernization
Union Bank Plaza
Los Angeles, California

1994
Gold Nugget Award of Merit
Office/Professional Building
Pasadena Towers
Pasadena, California

Progressive Architecture
Citation Award for Urban Design
A Greenway Plan for Metropolitan Los Angeles
Los Angeles, California

1993
Los Angeles Beautiful Business and Industry
Award for Architecture
SunAmerica Center/1999 Avenue of the Stars
Century City, California

Precast Concrete Institute
Special Recognition Award
William Morris Rodeo
Beverly Hills, California

Los Angeles Chapter AIA
Citation Award for Urban Design
A Greenway Plan for Metropolitan Los Angeles
Los Angeles, California

1992
Buildings, Facilities and Construction Management
Modernization Award, Buildings
Rincon Center
San Francisco, California

Gold Nugget Award of Merit
Best Community Site Plan
Leopalace Resort
Guam

Gold Nugget Award of Merit
Best New Town Land Plan
Ewa Town Center
Kapolei, Oahu, Hawaii

1991
Los Angeles Beautiful Business and Industry
Award for Architecture
Carnation Building/Nestlé USA Corporate
Headquarters
Glendale, California

1990
National AIA
Citation for Excellence in Urban Design
Highway 111 Corridor Master Plan
Indian Wells, California

1989
Progressive Architecture
Citation Award for Urban Design
Highway 111 Corridor Master Plan
Indian Wells, California

Los Angeles Chapter AIA
Citation Award for Urban Design
Highway 111 Corridor Master Plan and Specific Plan
Indian Wells, California

National AIA
Citation for Excellence in Urban Design
"Main Street," U.C. Irvine
Irvine, California

California Preservation Foundation
Award of Merit
Rincon Center
San Francisco, California

1988
Progressive Architecture
Citation Award for Urban Design
"Main Street," U.C. Irvine
Irvine, California

1987
California Council, AIA
Design Award
Ewa Town Center
Kapolei, Oahu Hawaii

Los Angeles Beautiful
Business and Industry Award
Fox Plaza
Century City, California

1986
West Los Angeles Chamber of Commerce
Beautification Award
Fox Plaza
Century City, California

RECENT PROJECTS

2003
Amgen Building 28
Thousand Oaks, California
Amgen, Inc.

Amgen Building 41 / Parking Structure 8
Thousand Oaks, California
Amgen, Inc.

Amgen Parking Structure 7
Thousand Oaks, California
Amgen, Inc.

Axium International Office Building
Los Angeles, California
Axium International

Bear Stearns
Century City, California
Bear Stearns

Beijing World Trade Commercial Center
Beijing, China
Global Trade Mansion

Bravo
Burbank, California
NBC

Downtown Metro Site Master Plan
Los Angeles, California
City of Los Angeles

East Los Angeles College Two Parking Structures
East Los Angeles, California
Los Angeles Community College District

Genentech Building 33
South San Francisco, California
Genentech, Inc.

JPL Building 180
Pasadena, California
Jet Propulsion Laboratory

JPL Oak Grove Masterplan
Pasadena, California
Jet Propulsion Laboratory

LAUSD Oso Elementary School Conversion
Woodland Hills, California
Los Angeles Unified School District

LAUSD Hesby Middle School Remodel
Encino, California
Los Angeles Unified School District

Mills Mercati Generali
Rome, Italy
The Mills Corporation

Mission College Parking Structure
Sylmar, California
Los Angeles Community College District

NBC
Burbank, California
NBC

Pierce College Art Gallery
Woodland Hills, California
Los Angeles Community College District

Pierce College Technology Building
Woodland Hills, California
Los Angeles Community College District

Sijing Housing Master Plan
Sijing, China
Shanghai Tuny Investment (Group) Co., Ltd.

Tenet HealthSystems
Alhambra, California
Tenet Health Systems, Inc.

UC Santa Barbara Extended Learning Services Building / Parking Structure 3
Santa Barbara, California
The University of California

Genentech Building 32
South San Francisco, California
Genetech, Inc.

Genentech Masterplan
South San Francisco, California
Genetech, Inc.

International Financial Resource Center
Beijing, China
Beijing JianJ: TianRun Real Estate Development Co., Ltd.

KNBC/Telemundo News Room
Burbank, California
NBC

Nanjing Xianlin University Town Center
Nanjing, China
City of Nanjing

Pacific Arts Plaza @ Two Town Center
Costa Mesa, California
Commonwealth Partners

St. Andrew's Abbey
Valyermo, California
St. Andrew's Abbey

Sunkist Corporate Headquarters
Sherman Oaks, California
Sunkist

United States Postal Service Retail Facility
Los Angeles, California
United States Postal Service

Zhongguancun International School
Haidian, Beijing, China
Topeak

2001
The Alhambra
Alhambra, California
The Ratkovich Company

Amgen Corporate Fitness Center
Thousand Oaks, California
Amgen, Inc.

The Donum Estate Winery
Sonoma, California
The Donum Estate / Racke USA

LA Center Studios Interiors
Los Angeles, California
LA Center Studios

LAUSD Central High School No. 10
Los Angeles, California
Los Angeles Unified School District

LAUSD East Valley Middle School No. 1
North Hollywood, California
Los Angeles Unified School District

Metropolitan Lofts
Los Angeles, California
Forest City Residential West

Mills Piers 27, 29–31/ YMCA on the Bay
San Francisco, California
The Mills Corporation

Shanghai New Jiangwan Town
Shanghai, China
City of Shanghai

Solano County Government Center
Fairfield, California
County of Solano

UC Berkeley College of Engineering Masterplan
Berkeley, California
The University of California

UC Berkeley Davis Hall North Replacement
Berkeley, California
The University of California

UC Irvine Cal IT²
Irvine, California
The University of California

Wilshire Country Club Renovation
Los Angeles, California
Wilshire Country Club

2000
Beijing Central Business District
Beijing, China
City of Beijing

Fangshan University Town
Beijing, China
Topeak

Gallo Sonoma Estate Winery
Healdsburg, California
Gallo Sonoma Estate Winery

Infomart/Terminal Annex Adaptive Re-use
Los Angeles, California
Infomart

JPL Flight Projects Center
Pasadena, California
Jet Propulsion Laboratory

NBC Executive Offices
Burbank, California
NBC

Northern Gateway
San Jose, California
Legacy Partners

Sandy Lane Resort Golf Clubhouse
St. James Parish, Barbados
International Investment & Underwriting, Ltd.

1999
Amgen Building 38
Thousand Oaks, California
Amgen, Inc.

City National Bank Branch
Burbank, California
City National Bank

Carrier Center Adaptive Re-Use
Los Angeles, California
H & R Properties, REIT

Constellation Place
Los Angeles, California
JMB Realty Corp.

Experian Corporate Headquarters
Costa Mesa, California
Experian, Inc.

Native American Museum and Cultural Center
Oklahoma City, California
Oklahoma Native American Cultural
& Educational Authority

North Hollywood Mixed-Use Masterplan
North Hollywood, California
JARCO SLG&G

Pacific Corporate Towers
El Segundo, California
CB Richard Ellis

Playa Vista Library
Los Angeles, California
City of Los Angeles

Private Residence
Larchmont Village
Los Angeles, California

Private Residence
Los Altos Hills, California

1998
Amgen Building 30 Phase II
Thousand Oaks, California
Amgen, Inc.

Beverly Hills Visitor Center Program
Beverly Hills, California
Beverly Hills Cultural Center

Capitol Area East End Complex
Sacramento, California
State of California, Department of General Services

Ford Point Multi-use Development Plan
Richmond, California
Forest City Development

Private Residence
Rutherford, California

21st Century Insurance Corporate Headquarters
Woodland Hills, California
Tishman Warner Center Venture

Warner Bros. E-1 Office Building
Burbank, California
Warner Bros.

1997
Amgen Building 30 Phase I
Thousand Oaks, California
Amgen, Inc.

Century Plaza Hotel Renovation
Century City, California
CPH Properties Inc.

Private Residence
Malibu, California

Junipero Serra State Office Building
Los Angeles, California
Los Angeles State Building Authority

Natural History Museum
Los Angeles, California
Los Angeles County

Mission Bay Masterplan
San Francisco, California
Catellus Development Corporation

Mondavi Coastal Winery
Monterey County, California
Robert Mondavi Winery

Oxygen Media Sunset Offices
Hollywood, California
Oxygen Media

Union Station Development Plan
Los Angeles, California
Catellus Development Corporation

Valencia Town Center III
Valencia, California
Newhall Land & Farming Company

Warner Bros. International Recreation Enterprises
Glendale, California
Warner Bros.

1996

All Saints Parish Renovation
Beverly Hills, California
All Saint's Parish

Amgen Parking Structure 3
Thousand Oaks, California
Amgen, Inc.

Byron Winery
Santa Maria Valley, California
Byron Vineyard and Winery

Los Angeles Civic Center Enhancement Plan
Los Angeles, California
Los Angeles Civic Center Authority

Marlborough School Renovation
Los Angeles, California
Marlborough School

NBC Masterplan
Burbank, California
NBC

Queensway Bay Parking Structure
Long Beach, California
City of Long Beach

RAMA IX Square
Bangkok, Thailand
Praram IX Square, Ltd.

University of Science and Technology Masterplan
Pattaya, Thailand
University of Science and Technology

Valencia Town Center I
Valencia, California
Newhall Land & Farming Company

Valencia Town Center II
Valencia, California
Newhall Land & Farming Company

1995
1888 Century Park East
Century City, California
JMB Realty Corp.

Al Khobar Resort Hotel
Al Khobar, Saudi Arabia
Al-Obiayi Contracting & Maintenance

Amgen Building 27
Thousand Oaks, California
Amgen, Inc.

Amgen Masterplan
Thousand Oaks, California
Amgen, Inc.

DreamWorks SKG Masterplan
Los Angeles, California
Maguire Thomas Partners, DreamWorks SKG

Four Media Office Building
Los Angeles, California
Four Media Company

Los Angeles International Airport Masterplan
Los Angeles, California
City of Los Angeles

Patramas Adhiloka Oil Plaza
Jakarta, Indonesia
PT Patramas Adhiloka

Sunflower City
Bangkok, Thailand
The Sunflower Group

Warner Bros. Technical Operations Offices
Burbank, California
Warner Bros.

1994
Los Angeles Open Space: A Greenways Plan
Los Angeles, CA
Pacific Earth Resources

Nas Agana
Guam
Guam Airport Authority

NBC - Jay Leno Tonight Show Stage
Burbank, CA
NBC

Private Residence
St. Helena, CA

Union Bank Plaza Renovation
Los Angeles, CA
Equitable, NLI

Warner Bros. Bridge Building
Burbank, CA
Warner Bros.

Warner Bros. Telepictures Productions' Corporate Office
Burbank, CA
Warner Bros.

SCOTT JOHNSON, FAIA

WILLIAM H. FAIN JR., FAIA

One of the most highly regarded architects in Los Angeles, Scott Johnson is also one of the few architects who is well-known to the general public and the design profession alike. A prolific designer of residential, commercial and institutional building projects, a number of his best-known designs have been widely published and have become local landmarks, including three high-rise buildings in Century City, California, the Opus One and Byron wineries in the Napa Valley and Santa Barbara County, respectively; Rincon Center in San Francisco, and the new Capitol Area East End in Sacramento. Born in California and educated at Stanford University, the University of California at Berkeley and Harvard's Graduate School of Design, Johnson worked variously at The Architects Collaborative in Cambridge, Mass., Skidmore Owings Merrill and the office of Philip Johnson and John Burgee in New York City. For the latter firm, he served as Design Associate for some of Johnson Burgee's most notable projects. During his tenure there, Scott Johnson also served as Assistant to Arthur Drexler in curating the "Three Buildings" exhibition at the Museum of Modern Art in New York(1981). Joining Pereira Associates in Los Angeles in 1983 as Principal and Design Director, he and William Fain acquired the firm now known as Johnson Fain in 1987. In addition to designing nearly 100 built projects in the past 16 years, Johnson has also taught at the Southern California Institute of Architecture, the USC School of Architecture, and the UCLA School of Art and Architecture. Active in the arts community, he is a Founder of the Museum of Contemporary Art in Los Angeles and serves as a board director of the Collage Dance Theatre , the Craft and Folk Art Museum, and a member of MOCA's Drawings Committee.

The Managing Partner of Johnson Fain Partners, Fain is also an Urban Designer with an international reputation and a long list of professional honors. Like Scott Johnson, Fain is a native Californian who took degrees from UC Berkeley (B.A.) and Harvard's Graduate School of Design (M.A.), also spending a year in-between to study at Manchester University in England. While still a graduate student at Harvard, Fain worked with Jacquelin T. Robertson as an Urban Designer in the Office of Midtown Planning & Development of New York City during the Lindsay administration. Continuing his work in the public sector, Fain served as Senior Architect and Urban Designer for the Boston Redevelopment Authority, and as a consulting urban designers on the downtown plan for Richmond, Va., and senior architect and urban designer for New Community Development Corporation in Washington, D.C. He joined Pereira Associates in 1980 as Director of Urban Design, and has served as Managing Partner for the firm since its inception in 1987. During his career, he has won two separate Fellowships from the National Endowment of the Arts and was the recipient of a Rome Prize Fellowships at the American Academy in Rome, Italy. He has taught at University of Southern California, Southern California Institute of Architecture and UCLA Extension.

PROJECT PARTICIPANTS

PARTNERS
Scott Johnson, FAIA *Design Partner*
William H. Fain, Jr., FAIA *Managing Partner,*
Urban Design/Planning

PRINCIPALS
Larry Ball, AIA *Project Management*
Juan Begazo, AIA *Urban Design/Planning*
Mark Gershen *Operations*
Dan Janotta, AIA *Design*
Patricia Shigetomi, AIA *Interiors*

SENIOR ASSOCIATES
Julie Bandini *Business Development*
Steve Levine, AIA *Urban Design/Planning*
Srinivas Rao *Urban Design/Planning*
Robert Shaffer, AIA *Urban Design/Planning*
Kevin Tyrrell, AIA *Architecture*
Greg Verabian, AIA *Architecture*

ASSOCIATES
David Alpaugh, AIA *Urban Design/Planning*
Morteza Alvani, AIA *Architecture*
Kristen Geraci *Marketing, Interior Design*
Neil Kaplanis, AIA *Interior Design*
Abhijeet Mankar, AIA *Architecture*
Carlo Paganuzzi, AIA *Architecture*
Jen Spangler, AIA *Architecture*
Suma Spina *Architecture*
Elena Valderrama *Finance & Administration*

FORMER ASSOCIATES
Jeffrey Averill
Christian Baker
Mark Gajda
Richard Gooding
Levin, Benjamin
Paul Murphey
Robert Pigati
Albert Sawano
Riccardo Tossani
Mark Zwagerman

COLLABORATORS
Brian Aamoth
Rodolfo Abrio
John Adams
Kimberly Aikman
William Akiyama
Yvonne Alexander
Morteza Alvani
Evelina Alvarez
Margot Alofsin
David Alpaugh
Eric Altizer
Farooq Ameen
M. Lourdes Amor
Natasa Andrejic
Magda Andreos
Stephen Andrew
Kenneth Arlt
Sherri Armstong
Lauri Arneson
Romeo Asprec
Marc Atkinson
Arturo Audelo
Richard Auton
Demetrios Avraamides
Jeffrey Averill

Alireza Badie
Amy Bailey
Christian Baker
Maria Baldenegro
Larry Ball
Julie Bandini
Ali Barar
Juan Carlos Begazo
Dolores Bell
Jason Bell
Dawn Bezzina
Neil Birnbrauer
Robin Bisbee
Thomas Blanchard
Daniel Blander
Robin Bloch
Venke Blyberg
Diana Bohan
Demetrio Boo
Jatesiri Boondicharern
Karen Boysen
Dale Bradbury
Tom Brakefield
Louis Bretana
Shari Brukman
G. Darcy Bruner
Sangeeta Bulani

Sandra Burga
Betty Burks
Aurora Bustamante

Carlito Calabia
Elizabeth Camayo
Ronald Cannan
Cynthia Carlson
Leah Carron
Jonathan Cantwell
Barbara Cass
Lisa Castro
Henry Chaikin
Christina Chan
Jonathan Chang
Hunvey Chen
Quin-Cheng Chen
Warren Chen
Judy Cheng
Henry Cheung
Tina Cheung
Vartan Cialichian
Janet Clifton
Kim Colin
Charles Cordero
Joanne Costello
Andrew Cox
Jerry Craig
John Crandell
Caleb Crawford
Charles Crawford
Jerry Craig
Chris Crolle
Joseph Cruz
Oscar de la Cruz
Timothy Cruz
Matthew Cummings
Victor Cusack

Jonathan DaDourian
Kershasp Dalal
John Danielian
Patric Dawe
David Decker
Philip De Cancio
Pearl Diggs
Jay Dimaggio
Nathalie Douge
David Du Mars

Lori East
Brenda Economides
Edmund Einy
Dan Elkins

Carmen Epstein
Elmer Evangelista
Johnathan Evans
Ronald Evitts

Davood Fakharian
Elizabeth Fain
Meg Fain
Janice Faucett
Michael Feinstein
Heidi Fichtenbaum
Clarence Fields
Joshua Fine
Carol Fisher
Editha Fortea
Irene Frankel
Sheri Frim
John Frost
Bruce Fullerton
Brent Fuqua
Marc Futterman

Garine Gabrielian
Mark Gajda
Arthur Garcia
Rigoberto Garcia
Christ Garness
Lilliana Gast
Soheir Georges
Kristen Geraci
Mark Gershen
Brent Gesell
David Gevers
Paula Giaconia
Leo Gomez
Richard Gooding
Kevin Gray
Richard Greenberg
Nina Gregory
Charles Grein
Jennifer Gridley
Gretchen Griner
Steve Grippentrog
Manuel Gonzales
Pablo Gonzalez
Pierpaolo Granata
Andreas Gritschke
Trina Gunther

Roddy Hames
Lauren Hammersley
Sherry Hammond
Carl Hampsn
Stephen Hanover

Mark Hembree
David Herrera
Vera Hetchel
Lisa Hill
John Hillbrand
Monica Himmelheber
Maricela Hinojosa
Megumi Hironaka
Adela Ho
Catherine Horrigan
Michele Hoye
Linda Hoyt
James Hsu
Mike Hsu
Henry Hua
David Huang
Mazie Huh
Marlin Hutchison

Nina Ifurung
Rumi Igrarashi
Laura Intscher
Rumi Igrarashi
Jennifer Iselin
Atsuko Itoda
Cameron Izuno

Adriana Mora Jackson
Warren Jacobs
Craig Jameson
    Dan Janotta

Barbara Kaplan
Neil Kaplanis
Amy Katz
Bette Kennedy
Mark Kim
Kyung Kim
Tricia Knopf
Michael Knopoff
Jacques Kravtchenko
Neil Kritzinger
Ivana Krstic
Jerry Kuriyama
Kurtiss Kusumoto
Daniel Kwok

Renato Lacson
Janie Huoy-Jen Lai
Roberta Lawry
Alistair Laws
Robert Lawson
Edward Lee
Jae Lee

Karl Lee
Loretta Lee
Benjamin Levin
Fernand Levin
Ben Levine
Stephen Levine
Jill Lewis
Benjamin Liao
Raleigh Lieban
Ning Lin
Vivian Lin
Brenda Lincoln
Judith Lippe
Sylvia S.T. Lo
Lizzy Loeb
Marci Loftin
Colins Lozada

Alex Macatula
Andrew Macliver
Anne Marie Madla
Christine Magar
Charles Magee
Kim Magner
Jerry Magnussen
Hung Mak
Kennis Mak
Wilfredo Manalo
Abhijeet Mankar
Noreena Manio
James Manning
Cheryl Marik-Toman
Molly Markert
Dean Martelli
John Martin
Maria Martinez
John Masotta
Gerhard Mayer
Shannon Rose Mcshea
James Meyer
Maryam Mims
Patrik Moccetti
Rodolfo Modina
Carmen Moore
Mark Moreno
Anita Moryadas
Paul Murphey

Andrew Naranjo
Risa Narita
Staci Nesbitt
Nick Nguyen
James Noh
Thomas Nohr

Dennis O'Meara
Rich Oechsler
Steven Oh
Timothy Oh
Michio Okamatsu
Jess Oliva
Rigoberto Ortega
Ronald Oster
Mark Owen

Carlo Paganuzzi
Diana Painter
Jennifer Pascoe
Blake Patten
Hui Yi Paterson
Calvin Peh
Alicia Perez
Cynthia Phakos
Chinh Pham
Kiet Phu
NinaPiaseckyj
Robert Pigati
George Plazony
Sandro Polo
Suzanne Porush
Teresa Powell
Haydee Prado
Medina Pruitt
Gig Pukprayura

Tuan Quach
Cesar Quinones
Roland Quirion

Mariam Rafigh
Raymond Rangel
Srinivas Rao
Victor Raskovsky
Dominic Rayner
Ian Remulla
Irlanda Rendon
Daniel Rhodes
Patty Rickles
Taina Rikala
Katherine Rinne
Lee Rivera
Alexander Rodak
Carol Rollins
Cheaseon Roh
Jacqueline Rosalagon
Debra Rosenbaum
Leslie Rowe
Kelly Ryan

Tsutomu Sakanaka
Amro Sallam
Orlando Sanchez
Nanette Sanger
Achille Santos
Albert Sawano
Jennifer Schab
Robert Schaffer
Heidi Schenker
Roy Schmidt
Jeffrey Sessions
Gavin Segal
Yogesh Seth
Sam Seymour, IV
Mark Shaw
Rocky Shen
Kevin Sherbrooke
Ritsuko Shibutani
Patricia Shigetomi
Sherry Shippy
Martin Simon
Yevgenty Slobodyanyuk
Roy Smith
Anson Snyder
Lisa Snyder
Joann Song
Leticia Soohoo
Jen Spangler
April Spease
Suma Spina
Tom Stallman
J. Odom Stamps
Edward Stavneak
Ralph Stanislaw
Margaret Starcevic
Ermias Stefanos
Henry Steinway
Jeffrey Stenfors
Malcolm Stiles
Roy Stuebinger
Wen-Chun Sun
F. Arnold Swanborn
Jan Szupinski

Warren Tamashiro
Kenji Tanaka
Diana Tasnadi
Beck Taylor
Charlotte Taylor
Leonard Temes
Wichai Thanavatik
Larry Tighe
Hung Ting
Warren Tomashiro

Gertrude Torres
Riccardo Tossani
Mark Tweed
Kevin Tyrrell
Burton Tysinger

Donna Vaccarino
Elena Valderama
Greg Verabian
Robert Vigeant
Robert Villagomez
Edito Villanueva
Dorian Viniegra
Janet Visconti-Clifton
Brad Vokes

Li-Hsin Wang
Phillip Warde
Breton Washington
Deborah Webster
Eric Weeks
Allan Weghorst
Yuming Wei
Aran Weng
Chris White
Nancy Wilksen
Michael Wilson
Stevens Wilson
Dianna Wong
Frank Wong
Andrea Woolf
Audrey Wu
Robert Wysinger

Alexander Yahontov
Donald Yamami
Sala Yao
Rose Yang
Yong-Kian Yeo
Alexander Yohontov
Alex Yoo
Sean Yun

Mahnam Zarrehparvar
Nazanin Zarkesh
Hraztan Zeitlian
Sarah Zimmerman
Chunyan Zhang
John Zorich
Mark Zwagerman

We wish to acknowledge the many and creative
contributions of consultants who are integral to all
our design efforts, including:

240

Abbie Gregg, Inc
Advanced Design Group, Inc
Affiliated Engineers, Inc. (AEI)
Associated Consulting Engineers Ltd
Athens Ent.
Aviation Systems Associates
Bard, Rao + Athanas (BR+A)
Bechtel Industrial
Boyle Engineering
Capital Engineering Consultants
Consensus Planning Group
Crosby Mead Benton
d'Auttemont-helms & Associates
David Ovich
Davies Associates
Dennis Brethel
Dickerson & Associates
DW Associates
Engineering Technology, Inc
Englekirk & Sabol
FBA Engineering
Flack + Kurtz
Forell/Elsesser Engineers
Frame Design
G.J. Fehlhaber
Gotama Building Engineers
Gotham Light & Power
Hanscomb Inc
Hargreaves Associates
Hayakawa Associates
Horton Lees Brodgen Lighting Design
HRP
HSI
Hunsaker & Associates
Innovative Engineering Group
International Parking Design
John A Martin & Associates, Inc
John M. Cruikshank and Associates
Judy Horton
JWDA, Shanghai
KCA Engineering, Inc
Kenderhall Enterprises Ltd
KL&A, Inc
Kocher & Schirra Consulting Engineers.
Korve Engineering
KPFF
Larkin Associates

Lawrence Moss Associates
Lea & Sung Engineering, Inc
Levine /Seegel Associates
Lighting Design Alliance
Lightvision
Linscott, Law & Greenspan
M3 Civil
MacKay & Somps
Martin & Huang
MB&A Mechanical Engineers
McNamara/ Salvia, Inc
ME Engineers
Melendrez Design Partners
Mia Lehrer Associates
Middlebrook + Louie
MPA Design
Nabih Youssef & Associates
Nancy Goslee Power and Associates
Ninyo & Moore
Olin Partnership
Ove Arup
Parker Resnick
Patsaouras & Associates, Inc
Peter Walker and Partners
PSOMAS
Public Works Design
R.E. Wall
Ralph Applebaum Associates
RBA Partners
Research Facilities Design (RFD)
Saiful/ Bouquet
Sanchez Kamps
SIKAND
Silver Roth
Simon Wong & Associates
Sussman/ Prejza & Company, Inc
SWA
Syska Hennessy Group
TKSC Mechanical Engineers
Tsuchiyama & Kaino
V & M Electrical Engineers
Veneklasen Associates
VLA Engineering, Inc
Vorgias Consulting
William J.Yang & Associates
Wilsey Ham
Wong Hobach Lau International